THE LORD GOD THE HEALER

He Healed Me From Cancers

Cyd Therese

TRILOGY CHRISTIAN PUBLISHERS
Tustin, CA

Trilogy Christian Publishers
A Wholly Owned Subsidiary of Trinity Broadcasting Network
2442 Michelle Drive
Tustin, CA 92780

The Lord God the Healer

For information, address Trilogy Christian Publishing

Rights Department, 2442 Michelle Drive, Tustin, Ca 92780.

For information about special discounts for bulk purchases, please contact Trilogy Christian Publishing.

Manufactured in the United States of America

10 9 8 7 6 5 4 3 2 1

Library of Congress Cataloging-in-Publication Data is available.

ISBN: 979-8-88738-019-3

ISBN: 979-8-88738-020-9 (ebook)

Dedication

This book is loving dedicated to the Lord God the Father, the Son Jesus Christ, and the Holy Spirit. I give all thanks to the Lord God Almighty for giving me this opportunity to experience His miraculous healing so I can share the message to His people that He is the Lord God the Healer.

Acknowledgements

I thank my husband, Joesel, who stood by me and uphold our wedding vows: "for better, for worse, for richer, for poorer, in sickness and in health, to love and to cherish, till death do us part."

I thank our daughters, Jo Trescha and Selcy Mae, for being there with me. I understand their pain and what they lost when I got sick. I believed that our Lord God Almighty will be there for you both as well for He loved you so dearly. You are both beautiful and precious in His sight. He is the Great Provider who will provide all that you need.

I thank my parents, Attorney Alaric Pena Acosta and Lydia Gongob Acosta, for bringing me up to know our God—Father, Son Jesus Christ, and Holy Spirit. This was the greatest gift I received from them which is worth far more than gold, silver, and rubies.

I thank my sister Annemarie, my three younger brothers and their families, my in-laws, all my extended families, and friends whom I encountered throughout my life at home, neighborhood, church, school, and work around the world. Your love, support, encouragement, and care strengthened me. You are truly a blessing to me. You helped me walk each step of my healing journey here on this beautiful world. You all helped me become the woman that God called me to be and achieve my purpose in life. I love you all. God bless you more abundantly.

Disclaimer

This book is intended to share my personal experiences in my cancer healing journey. I believe in the power of the Lord God the Healer and the Scriptures. The results of the healing journey teachings will come based on the belief and the relationship between each person and the Lord God the Healer (Exodus 15:26).

This book contains ideas and opinions from the author for informational and educational purposes only. This book is not intended to offer you medical advice. It should not be used to diagnose or treat any diseases. For the diagnosis or treatment of any medical or psychological issues, consult a licensed physician or psychiatrist, respectively.

References are provided for informational purposes only and do not constitute an endorsement of any books, websites, or other sources. Readers should be aware that the websites listed in this book might change.

Contents

Introduction

My name is Cyd Therese. I am a Christian: a follower of Jesus Christ, the Son of the One and Only True God, the God of Abraham, Isaac, and Jacob. I accepted Jesus Christ as my Savior, Lord, Master, Provider, and Healer. After the prompting of the Holy Spirit, I wrote this book to declare that the Lord God is the Lord God the Healer.

On February 2014, I was diagnosed with renal carcinoma that resulted in the removal of my right kidney. My diagnosis was similar to a diagnosis that my mother, Lydia Gongob Acosta, received in April 1997. After the surgery, she lived a normal life with no chemotherapy. The cancer never recurred until her death in May 2010. I prayed to my Lord God that He will heal me, comfort me, and be at my side all the time. My Lord God assured me and said, "I am the Lord God, your Healer."

After nine months from the kidney cancer diagnosis, I had a follow-up computerized tomography (CT) scan done by my oncologist. My oncologist told me that the CT scan showed a lymph node on my right lung. I was by myself and scared at that time. My oncologist said to me that he can see that I am already scared. He recommended a biopsy to confirm if it is cancer. He was hoping that it would not be aggressive like my previous kidney cancer or other lung cancers. I told him, "I am not going to be opened up again." He responded, "You looked good, physically. I will schedule you for a follow-up check in six months."

I was devastated when I stepped out of my oncologist's examination room. I found out more details after I got the copy of the CT scan result at the receptionist area. There was not just a lymph node on my right lung. Some cysts already developed on my liver and the remaining left kidney. Since the cancer cells were found in several organs, it was a "probable metastatic lung cancer." The right lung, liver, and remaining left kidney were all clear nine months earlier. I was in panic. Immediately I felt like I was taken in a roller coaster ride inside a dark cave. I felt butterflies inside my stomach as my heart began to beat faster. The adrenaline caused my body to tense. I was sweating all over my body. I wanted to scream so loud. The roller coaster ride seemed to last forever. I let go and allowed the Lord God to take over. Then suddenly it slowed down. It was like a welcomed friend, reminding me that it was over, to relax, and to get back to life. I was hesitant to go back to my oncologist office and ask for more explanations. Fear already engulfed me at this time. I had so many questions. How much time do I have left—three months, six months, one year? I was not prepared to hear any sad news anymore. That explained why I was getting weaker after the surgery in February 2014. I never regained back the energy. I cried out to the Lord my God. I was not prepared to face another cancer. This was new to me.

I asked the Lord God why I had two cancers in one year. The Lord God answered,

> "I want to show My people that I Am the Lord God the Healer." The Lord God assured me again, "I am the Lord God, your Healer. I heal you again, and again, and again."

I surrendered everything to Him. God is in control. I listened to the Holy Spirit for directions, leading, and guidance. I listened to His Words. I obeyed His Words. The God of Abraham, Isaac, and Jacob: He is my Lord, my God, my Heavenly Father, my Savior, my Provider, my Creator, my Rock, my Strength, my Great Shepherd, my Redeemer, my Salvation, and my Healer. I put all my trust in Him.

One night in July 2015, the pain attacked me again. I cried out to the Lord God Almighty to end my pain and suffering, for my heart could not take it anymore. Suddenly, I saw a light shining as bright as the morning sun. It was the shining hands of the Lord God reaching out to me. With both of my hands, I reached out for the hand of the Lord God quickly and placed it on top of the right side of my stomach, near the liver. Immediately, the pain was gone. What a miracle!

A few weeks later, I had a follow-up CT scan. My husband Joesel accompanied me at the oncologist's clinic to review the results in August 2015. The oncologist, Dr. Kapoor, smiled looking at my CT scan results. He looked at me and said, "Your CT scan is beautiful. There is no more trace of cancer." Hallelujah! Praise my Lord God, my Healer!

The Lord God keeps telling me to share my miraculous healing journey. I wrote this book to tell my story that the Lord God is the Lord God, my Healer. He is also your Healer. I pray that you will be encouraged and strengthened as you read this book, whether you are the person fighting the battle, or a family member, or a friend, or a caretaker of a person who is fighting the cancer battle or any battle against all kinds of sicknesses and diseases.

Remember the promise.
The Lord God is our Lord God, our Healer.

PART I:

THE BATTLES AND VICTORIES OVER CANCERS

CHAPTER 1

The First Cancer Diagnosis

It started on the morning of February 10, 2014. My urine was all colored pinkish red. I thought it was just my menstruation coming back after a three-month absence. It happened again the next morning. I remembered my Papa Alaric's issues with his kidney and bladder when I was a child and my mother's bout with kidney cancer when I was already a mother with two daughters in 1997. I was frantically scared, and my blood pressure started to rise. I prayed to my Lord God that it will not be anything major like my parents. I immediately called my general practitioner, a San Antonio Internal Medicine Specialist, Dr. Senger, MD, for consultation. He confirmed through urinalysis that there was indeed blood in my urine. He scheduled me for a CT scan that Friday, February 14, 2014. By Monday the following week, he called to inform me that he was referring me to a good San Antonio urologist for further examination and said nothing about the results of the CT scan. I was already anxious at that time and was wondering why he withheld that information.

Before the first diagnosis, I noticed something growing on my lower right abdomen a couple of years earlier. I went to the same doctor for diagnosis. I was referred to an obstetric gynecologist for further testing and diagnosis. The doctor ordered a sonogram of my lower abdomen due to the history of my left ovarian cysts in the past. The sonogram result was normal. As the days and months passed, I still noticed it growing. I remembered it exactly as when I was carrying my two daughters inside my womb. Nine months passed, and it still kept growing. The pain was bearable. As the months went by, I could easily dismiss the pain. The pain came and went; it became a part of my daily routine.

My husband Joesel drove me to the urologist's clinic for consultation that Wednesday, February 19, 2014. When we parked our car outside the clinic, my heart started pumping fast, for in front of us was a cancer center. I was not prepared to hear the news of cancer. I remembered not getting out of the car immediately. I was hoping it was just a dream. I needed a few minutes to collect myself. I prayed to my Lord God that He would be with me and strengthen me as I met the doctor, and that He would guide the doctor in the procedures and treatments to be done. When we went inside the clinic, the receptionist asked for all my medical information.

Then we were requested to wait in the waiting area. I noticed that most of the patients were male. The wait was short. We were finally called to see the urologist, Dr. Tecuanhuey, MD. He was a doctor in his seventies who reminded of my own Papa Alaric. Dr. Senger assured me that he is the best urologist and surgeon in his field in the San Antonio area. Somehow it gave me some peace and comfort. The urologist showed us the results of the CT scan. He said that there was a tumor which was half the size of the right kidney. He recommended immediate surgery. I told him of my Mommy Lydia's kidney cancer history. I told him that I was prepared to have surgery. Before he decided for the surgery, he asked me to come back the next day with the digital versatile disc (DVD) of the CT scan results. My husband, Joesel, and I went back the following day bringing the DVD of the CT scan from the Radiologist. As we watched the DVD, the urologist confirmed the size of the tumor which was half the size of the kidney. He said that it was encapsulated, which meant that it did not affect any other organ of my body. It was the same diagnosis as my Mommy Lydia. The tumor was also encapsulated on her kidney and did not affect the other organs. I was relieved and was full of hope of the diagnosis. The urologist recommended immediate surgery the following Tuesday, February 25, 2014.

The Grieving Process - At that time of receiving the news of kidney cancer, I was not prepared of the medical diagnosis. I was in denial. Maybe this was not happening. Maybe this was just a dream. Maybe not at my age, for I was ten years younger when my Mommy Lydia had the kidney cancer. Maybe there was a mistake on the CT scan reports. Maybe that urologist made a mistake on the diagnosis. I was initially angry with myself for not taking care of my body. I already knew of the cancer risk in my family, so why was I not taking any necessary precautions? What did I miss? My anger went on and on. Then I remembered the Bible verse about anger. "'In your anger do not sin.' Do not let the sun go down while you are still angry and do not give the devil a foothold" (Ephesians 4:26-27).

I immediately cried out to the Lord God asking Him for forgiveness for any sins that I knew I was doing and sins that I did not know I was doing. Then I started talking to the Lord God. I specifically asked the Lord God for forgiveness on disobedience. I told the Lord God that I will move to the Philippines to build the hospital that He had mentioned earlier in November 2012.

I was filled with grief and my spirit was low. I had been hospitalized three times in my forty-nine years of existence; twice for giving birth to my two beautiful daughters, Trescha and Selcy, and once for the removal of cysts in my left ovary. What would happen to me before, during, and after the surgery? There were a lot of emotions flooding into my being. The main emotion was fear: fear of death, fear of judgement from other people, fear of generational curses, and more. My blood pressure started to rise steadily. My internist gave me some medications to lower my blood pressure before surgery. I was worried that I would not survive during surgery. I was worried about what would happen to me after surgery. Would I regain my energy back? Then I remembered the Lord God, my Healer who healed me again, and again, and again. I accepted what was happening to my right kidney.

I asked the Lord God the Healer,
"Why cancer?"
The Lord God the Healer replied,
"I want My people to know that
I am the Lord God the Healer."

The Lord God the Healer's words brought assurance and great comfort. The battle was the Lord's, according to I Samuel 17:47. I believed that I had victory in the name of Jesus Christ of Nazareth, who died for me on the cross at Calvary. I started reaching out to my brothers and sisters in Christ. I first called my brother, Dr. Aldric G. Acosta, who was an internal medicine doctor and confirmed the results of the CT scan. He suggested that I have it removed immediately since it had not metastasized to the other organs. He assured me that I would live a normal life like my mother, with one kidney after the surgery. I also called my older sister, Annemarie, and told her about my medical condition. I told her that I was eating a lot of peanuts with my husband a couple of weeks before there was urine in my blood. I also told her that I already felt a dull pain on my lower left abdomen for more a couple of years. I had an ultrasound to confirm that there was nothing to be alarmed about. My sister told me of a similar incident with my mother eating peanuts before the kidney cancer diagnosis. I told a friend at work about the peanuts, and he said the aflatoxins in the peanuts could cause cancer. Now I knew that there were certain foods that were not good for the kidney that I should avoid. My sister, Annemarie, and brother, Aldric, assured me that it was okay to remove the right kidney just like our Mommy Lydia. We prayed and believed that our Lord God would heal me completely. My younger brother Jose who was in Australia also called me. He told me that they were praying for me at his church in Sydney. He was also kind to talk to my daughters and gave them comfort and assurance that everything would be alright with their mother. He told a similar story when our Mommy Lydia had cancer and the feeling that he felt as her son. He assured them that the Lord God would heal me. I called my oldest daughter, Trescha, who was in Dallas and informed her of the surgery. She flew to San Antonio the following Monday. At work, I asked my bosses for a leave of absence for approximately six weeks or more for I was scheduled for surgery the next week. My brother-in-law, Marjoe, and sister-in-law, Stella, from Houston visited us that weekend before the surgery. Another family friend, Lorna, also came to visit my in-laws. I informed them of my medical situation. I also called a good friend from my Philippine hometown, Eppie, a nurse by profession, and asked her a favor if she can come after work at the hospital to support my husband, Joesel, and my youngest daughter, Selcy. That Sunday, my husband, Joesel, and I met our Cornerstone Church Simeon Tribe Leader, Tom, and we asked him to pray for me before surgery. After church that Sunday, I was at peace in my soul and spirit. I was ready to face what my Lord God has prepared for me in the coming days.

CHAPTER 2

God's Commission

Before I was diagnosed with the kidney cancer, the Lord God spoke to me fifteen months earlier. In November 2012 as I was driving to work that morning, the Lord God spoke to my spirit as I passed by the North Central Baptist Hospital and said,

"Build me a hospital in the Philippines."
I simply answered, "I am not a doctor, Lord."
And the Lord God answered,
"I will teach you."

Then I realized that it was the Lord God speaking. I did not know what to do at that time. Do I have to leave everything and go back to the Philippines? Do I have the necessary skills and resources? My work experience background was in accounting, audit, business, financial, and information technology in different financial services, manufacturing, oil and gas, retail, and other industries, but not a medical industry. What about my husband Joesel and our two daughters who were both in college at that time? In the days that followed, the Lord God always told me, "Watch Joesel." At that time, Joesel and I were cell leaders at John Hagee's Cornerstone Church in San Antonio, Texas. We were under the Simeon Tribe with our leaders Tom and Linda and John and Carmen. During our Friday cell meeting prayer time, I asked Joesel for any prayer request. He and the other members requested healing, provisions, and guidance.

Then on Saturday morning on November 10, 2012, my husband Joesel woke up early and prepared breakfast. He cooked his favorite Filipino breakfast: fried rice, eggs, and dried squid from the Philippines. Breakfast was great that morning. Joesel and I enjoyed breakfast with our youngest daughter, Selcy. Our oldest daughter, Trescha, was in nursing school at Baylor University in Dallas, Texas. After breakfast, I told Joesel that I had some work to finish online. Yes, we already had work from home (WFH) capability at that time at USAA. Our daughter Selcy also went to her room. Joesel stayed in the family room watching television. After a few minutes, Joesel said that he will work on something outside. He did not specify what he was going to work outside. Then the Holy Spirit spoke again and said, "Watch Joesel." I kept looking from the computer room door upstairs to our front yard. I noticed that the tree in our front yard was swaying. I did not go outside to check Joesel. I just went back to work on my computer. Then after a few minutes, Joesel came back inside and shouted for me to come down to the family room immediately. As I hurried downstairs, the first thing I thought was that he had an accident with what he was doing with the tree in the front yard. However, when I got downstairs, Joesel was already laying down on the family room sofa drenched wet with sweat. He could hardly breathe. He told me to change and take him to the emergency room. I was still calm at this time; I did not even hurry to get changed. I still took time to take a shower before changing. My daughter Selcy told me later why I was taking things calmly in the time of emergency. In my spirit, I knew the Lord God was with us. He was in control of everything. I placed everything in His hands.

When I went downstairs to check on Joesel, he said that we had to wait for the ambulance. He said that it was better to call 911 for the ambulance because he had a heart attack. Yes, he was definitely right. It allows the medical community nearby to find the best facility and doctors to take care of him. The ambulance came a few minutes later. Two men came to assess Joesel's situation. They were asking for aspirin, but we did not have aspirin at the house. Then we waited for the firetruck to come. Three more men arrived. They had aspirin this time. After giving Joesel aspirin and confirming which hospital to send him to, they immediately carried him to the ambulance. Thank God that Joesel was sent to the nearest hospital, North Central Baptist, about one mile away from our house. This was the same hospital where the Lord God told me to build Him a hospital in the Philippines. I remembered being scared and nervous riding in the front of the ambulance. When we arrived, it seems like the whole emergency department was waiting for Joesel. They brought him to the room and cut off his clothes with a pair of scissors. They changed Joesel to hospital clothes. Then they performed more tests. My daughter Selcy later arrived. We were asked to stay outside in the waiting room. Later Dr. Moore, MD, came and talked to Selcy and me. He said that Joesel had a massive heart attack. All the major arteries were clogged. He and his medical team would perform a bypass on the last major artery that they suspected caused the heart attack. After more than an hour, Dr. Moore came back to us at the emergency waiting room. He said, "The surgery was successful. You can visit your husband once he is moved to the Intensive Care Unit (ICU)." Joesel was later moved to the ICU in the afternoon. While Joesel was resting in his room, he suddenly felt like he was drowning. I called the nurse and asked the doctor for assistance. Later Joesel was diagnosed with congested heart failure. The next day, the two ICU nurses asked me about Joesel's condition. They showed me the results of his X-ray tests. It was a massive heart attack.

They said, "We have not seen a patient survived a massive heart attack like him.
It is truly a miracle from God."
It was indeed a miracle that Joesel survived.
I give the Lord God all the glory, honor, and praise for healing my husband Joesel.

While in the hospital, I told the Lord God that I accepted His commission to build Him a hospital in the Philippines. I also accepted His way of teaching me how the hospital will be built and how the hospital business works. I asked Him to give me knowledge and wisdom to design and operate a hospital the way He wants it to be, according to His perfect will in His perfect time. Praise the Lord! Hallelujah!

A few months earlier, I asked the Lord God about His plan for my life, especially my career. I had worked at USAA for more than a decade already. As I was walking at the courtyard outside my office desk, the Lord God spoke to me. I was in front of the wall or arch in the middle of the courtyard. The Lord God said, "You are here to learn." USAA is a financial services association serving the members of the US Armed Forces and their families. I started working at the investment management company as a fund accountant in June 1998. After two years I joined the Internal Audit Department where

I remained until I retired in February 2015. I audited the different areas of the company from corporate finance, operations, real estate, information technology (IT), property and casualty insurance, life insurance, and more. I performed financial, operations, and IT audits. I was also involved in project management especially in the area of IT. I understood what the Lord God meant that I was there at USAA to learn. USAA had humble beginnings and impressive successes. It started as an auto insurance to help military officers. To date, it has grown to serve millions in the US Armed Forces and their families both active military duty and retirees. My educational background is in accounting and I have a master's in business administration. My work experiences brought me around the world from working at SyCip, Gorres, Velayo, & Company (SGV & Co.) in Makati, Philippines, to working with audit clients in the Philippines and in Seoul, South Korea. I also worked at a carpet business in Germany, and companies in Houston and San Antonio, Texas, USA. I knew my educational background and work experiences helped me prepare for a great task to build the Lord God, our Healer a hospital in the Philippines.

Our daughter Trescha flew back to San Antonio to visit her dad Joesel. Our church families from Cornerstone Church (the families of Larry and Joy, June and Judith, Randy and Madeline, Ate Lolet, Chris and Gemma,

Jon and Carmen, Tom and Linda) and Lord of the Harvest Church (the families of George and Angelita, Don and Annie, Ron and Lucy, Steve and Carmelita, Kevin and Cathy, and Eppie) also visited to give us support. Another friend, Laura, from Organization of Filipinos in Texas visited us. My co-workers, Cathy and Tuyet, also visited and brought some gifts from the whole audit team. The visitors' presence strengthened and helped us lightened some of our burdens. It was pure joy seeing them at the hospital showing their support. On the fifth day, Joesel was moved to a regular two-bed room. Then Joesel was finally released from the hospital on Thursday, November 15, 2014.

Joesel's family from Houston (Dad Jose, Mom Sela, sister, and brother with his wife and children) came and visited us that weekend to celebrate Thanksgiving.

A couple of months later in February 2013, the doctor implanted a defibrillator in Joesel. It was a one-hour outpatient surgery. However, due to Joesel's history of heart attack, the doctor recommended that he should stay overnight at the hospital for observation. Joesel was released the following day. He was recovering well over the next few months. Joesel was able to go back to work in April 2013. Truly, God is a miracle-healing God. To God be the glory!

CHAPTER 3

Victory Over the First Cancer

The Lord God the Healer is the only One I knew and believed in my heart that would give me victory over cancer. He healed me and rescued me again, and again, and again, over sickness and death throughout my life.

Gift of Salvation - I accepted the Lord Jesus as my Lord, Savior, and Healer at a young age (about seven). I remember the night when I was running a high fever. I saw a witch dressed in a long black gown, with long black hair and black hat. The witch was chasing me up and down the balcony at my paternal grandparents', Leoncio and Petra Acosta, house in Oroquieta City. I was very afraid of the witch. I did not want the witch to catch me. After a while, I was very exhausted running away from the witch. I asked my Mommy Lydia to get the witch to stop chasing me. But she told me that there was no witch. My parents had a party that evening. We also had two medical physicians, Dr. E. Lumantas and

Dr. M. Fuentes, who were present that evening. I heard them telling my parents that if the fever would not go down, I could possibly die. I saw my sister Annemarie and another friend who peeped in the room. They were crying. I was pondering on the words I heard about death. I only saw our neighbors' grandma who had previously died. I told my parents that I visited the grandma's wake and even touch her cold body. I asked my parents what happens when a person dies. They told me about heaven and hell. But I never fully understood it at that time. After a while, I no longer had energy to run away from the witch. I was devastated that neither my parents nor the doctors could help me. I was desperate and helpless. I didn't have anybody to help me. Then I remembered my paternal grandma, Petra Pena Acosta, who told me,

"Bad girls go to hell. Good girls go to heaven."

In my spirit, I thought that this must be the witch who would take people to hell. It was my time to die. Then I remembered from Sunday school that the Lord Jesus Christ died on the cross at Calvary to take away the sins of the world and give people eternal life. Then I called on the name of the Lord Jesus Christ to forgive me of all my sins.

"Lord Jesus, hear my prayer.
I am like the thief who asked You to take him
to paradise with You.
Forgive me of all my sins.
Lola Petra said I am a bad girl.
I don't want to go with the witch to hell.
Take me with You to heaven.
Lord Jesus, if You heal me,
I will serve You all the days of my life."

Then suddenly, the witch was gone. My fever was gone. The next thing I remembered was the next morning. I was walking to school. Then I remembered what the Lord Jesus Christ had done for me. He heard my prayer: He healed me and delivered me from the witch. I was so amazed at the Lord Jesus Christ that He listened to a child like me. I am amazed by the *power of the name of Jesus Christ*. I was so blessed to receive a supernatural healing.

That day, I believed that the Lord God the Father, the Son, and the Holy Spirit, who we worship in church is a living, mighty, and powerful God. Hallelujah!

Later as an adult, I continued to remember that, as a child of God, I can call on His name in time of need. The Lord God can heal me from cancer. I again called on the name of the Lord Jesus Christ. I then declared in my spirit that the Lord God is my Savior, Master, and Healer. I surrendered everything to Him. I know that the Lord God was in control of my life. I trusted Him completely. I believed in Him. I put all my whole faith in Him. My Lord God assured me and said,

"I am the Lord God, your Healer.
I heal you again and again."

Gift of Faith - My Papa Alaric and Mommy Lydia both believed and accepted our Lord Jesus Christ as their Lord and Savior. Both my mother and father introduced their children to the Lord Jesus Christ. They faithfully brought all five children to Oroquieta Evangelical Church in our hometown of Oroquieta City, Philippines. My father also brought all the other cousins who lived in the Acosta family compound. I remembered asking him one time why we had to go to church every Sunday. He answered,

"The church is like a hospital for the sinful and the sick. The people get tired from the work and labor for working six days. On the seventh day, we all go to church to get our healing, deliverance, and restoration. Then we will be refreshed and renewed for the next week."

We grew up with no health insurance. I was never hospitalized when we were growing up. I was just amazed at the great and powerful Lord God that we worship in church, that He makes us all healthy. I am grateful for my parents for grounding us in the faith of the One True God, the God of Abraham, Isaac, and Jacob, and His Only Son our Lord Jesus Christ, and the Holy Spirit.

> Now to each one the manifestation of the Spirit is given for the common good. To one there is given through the Spirit a message of wisdom, to another a message of knowledge by means of the same Spirit, *to another faith by the same Spirit,* to another gifts of healing by that one Spirit, to another miraculous powers, to another prophecy, to another distinguishing between spirits, to another speaking in different kinds of tongues, and to still another the interpretation of tongues. All these are the work of one and the same Spirit, and He distributes them to each one, just as He determines.
>
> 1 Corinthians 12:7-12

Papa Alaric and Mommy Lydia bought us a huge picture English Children's Bible. I usually sat down in a room next to my Papa Alaric's law office and read the Bible. I would go through the Bible stories. I called Papa Alaric or Mommy Lydia to explain to me some of things that I didn't understand in English or anything that required spiritual maturity. I loved all the Bible stories. I am amazed in the power of the Holy Spirit to help us understand His love for all of us created beings. I was encouraged by the different people in the Bible who shared their faith in God. "Consequently, faith comes from hearing the message, and the message is heard through the word about Christ" (Romans 10:17).

The Surgery - On Tuesday, February 25, 2014, at eight in the morning, my husband Joesel and our oldest daughter Trescha brought me to Baptist Medical Center in downtown San Antonio for surgery. Trescha had flown in from Dallas, where she was studying at the Louise Herrington School of Nursing at Baylor University. After completing all the paperwork at the hospital check-in counter, I was placed into a wheelchair and prepped for surgery. I changed into a hospital gown. They checked all my vital signs. I was then ushered into the surgery pre-operation area. I would have two procedures. The first one was to freeze my kidney to reduce bleeding. It took one hour, and I was awake for this procedure. I didn't feel the pain, but I felt that my body was freezing and shivering. After the procedure, I was rushed back again to the pre-operation area, where I was given anesthesia before the surgery. I saw my husband Joesel and my daughter Trescha before surgery. I heard my urologist, Dr. Tecuanhuey, asking for my whereabouts and status as he was walking in the hallway. Then I slipped into a deep sleep. That was around two in the afternoon. The next time I woke up was around seven in the evening, I was already in the Intensive Care Unit (ICU). My urologist had awakened me from my sleep. I tried to complete my sentence that I had started earlier with my oldest daughter Trescha when we were in the pre-operation area. Then I realized that she had already flown back to Dallas. My youngest daughter Selcy was with me at this time. She had school at the University of Texas at San Antonio (UTSA), so she was not able to come with us in the morning. My urologist told us that the surgery went well. The tumor and the right kidney were removed. My husband Joesel was there too. Two of our good friends, Eppie and Ginah, from my hometown, Oroquieta City, Philippines, were also there when I awoke from surgery. Eppie, a nurse by profession, was at the hospital after my surgery to give support to my husband Joesel and to explain any medical terms that he might not understand. Joesel also had his own battle with medical issues when he had a heart attack and a congested heart failure in November 2012. I did not want him to suffer any amount of stress. Eppie also called our good friend Ginah, a physical therapist by profession, to accompany her on her visit. I thank God that I woke up after the surgery and was surrounded by my husband, daughter, and friends.

Angel Nurses - After my urologist, husband, daughter, and friends left, the two nurses (male and female, one each side) were attending me at the ICU. Dr. Tecuanhuey explained that he made a special request that I be attended by two nurses to take care of me since I had a difficult surgery. He wanted me to be as comfortable as possible and make a speedy recovery. Surely, the two nurses took good care of me round the clock checking my vital signs, giving me sips of icy water, checking my intravenous (IV) bags, changing my urine bag regularly, checking the electrical compression device on my legs to prevent stroke, and making me comfortable as much as possible. God was good for sending me those two angel nurses to take care of me. I thank God for Dr. Tecuanhuey who made my hospital stay comfortable.

Overcoming the Spirit of Death - By ten in the evening, my spiritual battle began. I could sense in my spirit the spirit of death hovering around the ICU and outside my room. I knew that the Lord my God would walk with me as I went through the valley of death. I remembered Psalm 23.

> The Lord is my Shepherd; I shall not want. He maketh me to lie down in green pastures: He leadeth me beside the still waters. He restoreth my soul: He leadeth me in the paths of righteousness for His name's sake. *Yea, though I walk through the valley of the shadow of death, I will fear no evil: for Thou art with me; Thy rod and Thy staff they comfort me. Thou preparest a table before me in the presence of mine enemies: thou anointest my head with oil; my cup runneth over.* Surely goodness and mercy shall follow me all the days of my life: and I will dwell in the house of the Lord forever.
>
> Psalm 23 (KJV)

I also remembered the Israelites on the Passover night. Immediately I called on the name of my Lord Jesus Christ. I declared and commanded,

"In the name of Jesus Christ of Nazareth,
spirit of death get out of my life and my room.
The blood of Jesus is in the door post of my soul.
No harm can come to me."

I repeated these words of declaration again, and again, and again for a couple of minutes. I stood on the Word of God as mentioned in the Bible.

> And they shall *take of the blood and strike it on the two side posts and on the upper door post of the houses*, wherein they shall eat it...For I will pass through the land of Egypt this night and will smite all the firstborn in the land of Egypt, both man and beast; and against all the gods of Egypt I will execute judgment: I am the Lord. And *the blood shall be to you for a token upon the houses where ye are and when I see the blood, I will pass over you, and the plague shall not be upon you to destroy you,* when I smite the land of Egypt.
>
> Exodus 12:7, 12-13 (KJV)

After a few minutes, I heard a commotion at the patient's room next-door. Everyone in the ICU ran to assist the patient in the next room, including my two attending nurses. After a few more minutes, they declared the patient brain dead and called the family. My thoughts and prayers went to the patient and the families. I prayed that the Lord God would comfort them and give them peace. I gave my Lord God, my Healer all the glory, honor, and praise. I knew deep in my heart that He was declaring in my life that He was the Lord God the Healer. I thank my Lord God for protecting my life that evening. Hallelujah!

Truly there was power in the name of Jesus and by the blood of Jesus.

The Hospital Recovery - After two days in the ICU, I was transferred to a private room at the hospital. The breathing tube was removed. The catheter was also removed. This time, I did not have two dedicated nurses, but different hospital staffs were checking on me every hour such as the attending nurses, the respiratory therapists, the nurse assistants, the food attendants, the cleaning crew, and the doctors. I thank the Lord God for their dedication and passion for their jobs in helping me heal and recover quickly at the hospital. By Thursday evening, I was able to walk out of the bed to the toilet. By Friday, I was able to walk in the hallways. My stomach started to bloat Friday afternoon for I was not able to fart yet. I did not know how important farting was until that day after the surgery. My urologist said that I would not be able to go home until I farted. By Saturday, I gladly told my urologist that I was able to fart. My urologist said that I could go home by Sunday evening. Hallelujah!

The Visitors and Gifts – Family and friends were important in the healing and recovery of a patient. Although we only requested one friend Eppie to come and support Joesel, other friends also came to visit me and my family (Joesel, Trescha, and Selcy) at the hospital. I had twelve friends who visited: Eppie, Ginah, Marlene (another friend from my hometown), Tom and Linda (our church Simeon tribe leaders), Lorna (a good friend I met as a young military wife on base in Germany), Yany and Rick (another friend), and our church cell group family of Joy and Larry with their two children. Their visits helped me tremendously to recover quickly. They gave me gifts, words of hope, encouragement, and strength. I also thank the Lord God for dozens of well-wishers on my husband Joe's Facebook page. My office co-workers at USAA Audit sent me a gift and a card. Another friend sent me a teddy bear nurse. Dozens of friends sent gifts, get-well cards, encouragement, and prayers.

> Then the King will say to those on his right, "Come, you who are blessed by my Father; take your inheritance, the kingdom prepared for you since the creation of the world. For I was hungry and you gave me something to eat, I was thirsty and you gave me something to drink, I was a stranger and you invited me in, I needed clothes and you clothed me, *I was sick and you looked after me,* I was in prison and you came to visit me."
>
> Matthew 25:34-36

Going Back Home Full of Hope - Praise the Lord! I was finally sent back home on Sunday evening after six days in the hospital. It was a great feeling to be alive and well. My hometown friends, Eppie, Elsa, and Dr. Noli, also came to visit, give me a gift, and pray for me. I continued to walk when I was at home. I had difficulty getting out of bed. But once I was out of the bed, I could walk by myself. I was slowly regaining strength on my right hip and leg. By the end of April, I was able to go back to work. Praise the Lord for healing and recovery!

> God's law was given so that all people could see how sinful they were. But as people sinned more and more, God's wonderful grace became more abundant. So just as sin ruled over all people and brought them to death, now God's wonderful grace rules instead, giving us right standing with God and resulting in eternal life through Jesus Christ our Lord.
>
> Romans 5:20-21 (NLT)

God's Abundant Grace - Truly, God's grace was abundant in my life after the surgery. It gave me the victory over cancer, over the unhealthy lifestyle, fear, doubts, unbelief, and other tests in life.

> Who then will condemn us? No one—for Christ Jesus died for us and was raised to life

> for us, and He is sitting in the place of honor at God's right hand, pleading for us. Can anything ever separate us from Christ's love? Does it mean He no longer loves us if we have trouble or calamity, or are persecuted, or hungry, or destitute, or in danger, or threatened with death? (As the Scriptures say, "For Your sake we are killed every day; we are being slaughtered like sheep.") No, despite all these things, overwhelming victory is ours through Christ, who loved us. And I am convinced that nothing can ever separate us from God's love. Neither death nor life, neither angels nor demons, neither our fears for today nor our worries about tomorrow—not even the powers of hell can separate us from God's love. No power in the sky above or in the earth below—indeed, nothing in all creation will ever be able to separate us from the love of God that is revealed in Christ Jesus our Lord.
>
> Romans 8:34-39 (NLT)

God's Amazing Love - God's love is amazing. It is pure and everlasting. God's love embraced me fully through all the trials in my life. Truly nothing can separate us from the love of God.

CHAPTER 4

The Second Cancer Diagnosis

Oncologist Follow-Up - My urologist referred me to an oncologist, Dr. Kapoor, MD, for follow-up checks on the kidney cancer. I first saw my oncologist in August 2014. He complimented me that I looked great. He said it was good that the cancer was encapsulated. He recommended seeing me in two months. Then on my second visit in October, he ordered a follow-up CT scan to check any recurrence of cancer before December 2014.

CT Scan - The week of Thanksgiving 2014, my two daughters, Trescha and Selcy, accompanied me at the Diagnostics Imaging Center for the CT scan. We prayed to the Lord God for good results. I was confident that the cancer will not recur like my mother. I remembered talking to the CT scan technician, and she sounded as if everything was alright.

Oncologist Reading of CT Scan Results - The first week of December, I went to visit my oncologist to discuss the CT scan results. I was alone this time and did not bother to ask my husband to accompany me. I was confident that everything would be okay. I remembered sitting alone at the oncologist's exam room. The oncologist walked into the exam room. He glanced at my medical records. Then he looked at me straight into my eyes. He calmly told me that CT scan showed a lymph node on my right lung. Immediately I got scared and was in panic mode. I was not expecting more bad news in less than a year. I was hoping that I would be healthy the remainder of my life. My oncologist told me that he could see that I was already scared. He was hoping that it would not be aggressive like the "other cancer." Wait, I had cancer? My urologist told us at the hospital that the result of the kidney biopsy was negative, and the tumor was not cancerous. So that was cancer after all? I remembered my follow-up check with my urologist where he asked me if I could be interviewed for the Latino television channel. I accepted the interview. My urologist introduced me, "This is Cyd, who survived kidney cancer. Her right kidney was removed." So it was cancer after all. I was shocked at that moment. I just received a death sentence, and I was alone at the oncologist's exam room. I was so helpless. I felt like my world around me was collapsing. I still heard my oncologist talking in the background. I barely understood what he was talking about. I was in shock. I asked, "What will be our next steps?" He replied, "I recommend a biopsy." I asked again, "Is it a form of treatment"? He answered, "It is another diagnostic test to confirm that it is cancer." Yes, I knew that. At that point, I just wanted to ask the oncologist to confirm things to make sure that I am not in a dream. I responded, "I do not need another diagnostic test to confirm it is cancer." He respected my decision. He complimented me and said, "You look great. I will see you in six months in June 2015. You can come back anytime if you need to see me." Hearing those words from my oncologist gave me hope.

Detailed CT Scan Results – I was devastated when I stepped out of my oncologist's examination room. I found out more after I got the copy of the CT scan at the receptionist area. There was not just a lymph node on my right lung. Several cysts had grown on my liver and the remaining left kidney. They were all clear nine months earlier. I was hesitant to go back to my oncologist office and ask for more explanations. Why did he only mention a nodule in the right lung? He did not mention about the cysts on the liver and the remaining left kidney. Or did I just miss this information when I initially spaced out when I heard about the lung nodule? Where did I get all these cancers? The CT scan results confirmed the reason why I was getting weaker after the kidney surgery early that year.

Lungs – I remembered a friend, Yvette, who died of lung cancer in 1991 seven months after the diagnosis. I never knew anyone who survived lung cancer. I knew my father had a history of lung disease. As a child, I was diagnosed with primary complex. I knew my lungs always needed support. Growing up, there was no smoking in our home. This was the reason that I never got into the habit of smoking. I also developed severe seasonal allergies as an adult when I moved to the big city in Manila. It eventually went away. But it came back after a couple of years living in San Antonio, Texas.

Kidneys - My mother survived the kidney cancer, and her one remaining kidney was healthy until her death in May 2010. My father also had some issues with his kidney and bladder when I was still a child. I always had issues with my urinary tract as an adult. Then the kidney cancer was diagnosed in February 2014. And now cysts were growing on my remaining left kidney? How will I survive without a healthy kidney?

Liver - I knew that my liver needed tender loving care. My liver did not respond well to strong medications. In 1995, I was treated after a positive result on the tuberculosis skin test in Fairchild Air Force Base hospital in Washington state. Growing up in the Philippines, we had a vaccine to prevent tuberculosis, thus it was possible to get a positive result. It did not mean that tuberculosis had developed. We discussed it with my doctors; the medication was stopped, and the liver pain was gone.

My Papa Alaric was diagnosed with those liver cysts in December 2008, and fourteen months later he passed away. I remembered the pain and agony that he suffered during those fourteen months. I initially visited him early January 2009 to discuss with him possible treatment. I remembered him telling me that he was already at peace with God, the Author and Finisher of our lives and his medical situation. He did not want to go to Manila or any other foreign cities that had cancer treatments at that time. He did not want to spend any more money or resources. In 2005, my fathered suffered from a disease on his spinal column that left him with physical disabilities. I can see the pain and burden that the liver cysts added to his condition. He was a strong man. I specifically remembered him crying painfully when I called him three days before he passed away. He said that the pain in his liver was getting worse, and it was too much for him to bear. I asked him to call my brother the medical doctor, his son Aldric, for any pain medications. We prayed that the Lord God strengthen him to endure the pain. Three days later, he died peacefully in his sleep. No more pain and no more tears. My Papa Alaric was finally reunited with our Creator. Praise the Lord!

Response to Cancer Diagnosis – Denial, Anger, Bargaining, Depression, Acceptance

I went through the five stages of grief in dealing with my cancer diagnosis, referring to Kubler-Ross: 1) denial, 2) anger, 3) bargaining, 4) sadness/depression, and 5) acceptance. The responses did not come in the order that it is presented. However, when any of the grief stages came, I dealt with it bravely by prayer, self-talk, encouragement, forgiveness, and surrendering everything to God.

Denial - I was prepared for a positive diagnosis after the kidney cancer surgery. My Mommy Lydia's kidney cancer did not recur until her death in 2010. I was hoping for the same diagnosis. When the oncologist told me that there was a recurrence, I was completely shocked. At first, I thought that it was a mistake. I did not accept the report from the CT scan report. I was in the stage of denial. I wanted to go back to the diagnostic company to validate that it was my CT scan. Maybe they had switched it with someone else's CT scan report. Maybe their machine was not working. Maybe my oncologist just read another patient's medical report. In my mind, metastatic lung cancer was deadly. Death was knocking again at the doorpost of my soul. I had so many questions. How much time do I have left, three months, six months, one year? I was not prepared to hear any more words. That explained why I was getting weaker after the kidney surgery earlier in the year. I never regained back the energy. I felt like a burning candle that had almost died out. I cannot explain that feeling, but the CT scan proved it. I did not know or understand cancer that much. But I knew that it was a deadly disease. I was in a state of shock and denial when all these questions flooded into my mind. I went numb. Then I remembered the Lord my God and cried out unto Him. I needed my Lord, my God, my Savior, my Healer, more than ever before at this stage. I was at the crossroad of my life. I did not know how to proceed with my life. I did not know what to tell my husband and children, my sister and brothers, and the rest of my family. I needed my Lord God's love and grace at that point.

Anger - I was initially flooded with anger towards myself. I was angry at myself that I did something wrong to make the cancer recur in less than a year. I did the cancer surgery just like my mom. The only difference was that I had the procedure to freeze the kidney to prevent it from bleeding. Maybe that was a mistake. The medicines they put into my body may have caused the cancer. I was angry at the decision I made earlier. However, later on, that anger was gone. I convinced myself that it was a good decision. I could have died earlier due to bleeding during surgery or complications like the other patient who died after the surgery.

I was also angry that I did not take care of my body well. I was angry that I did not pay attention to the symptoms of the disease when it was at the earlier stage before it metastasized. I felt that my doctors did not help me or guide me or lead me to live a life that was cancer free. I felt that the people around me did not help me or guide me or lead me to a state of wellness. Was it caused by the food I ate or any liquid I drank? There was a lot of blaming. As a teenager, I was diagnosed with juvenile arthritis and was bedridden for three days. To prevent the progress of the disease, I could not smoke or drink alcohol, and I was limited to certain kinds of foods. I also had tendencies to develop cysts in the past. After I delivered my first baby in 1991, I developed cysts in my left ovary that resulted to its removal (cystectomy). After I delivered my second baby in 1992, I started developing cysts in my breasts. But thank God, it went away. As a child, I was diagnosed with primary complex. I knew my lungs always needed support. I also developed severe seasonal allergies as an adult. That was why I had difficulty breathing on several occasions. How did it happen that I missed all the signs that my body was signaling me? My anger went on and on. Then I remembered, "'In your anger do not sin.' Do not let the sun go down while you are still angry, and do not give the devil a foothold" (Ephesians 4:26-27). I immediately cried out to the Lord God asking Him for forgiveness for any sins that I knew I was doing and that I did not know I was doing.

Bargaining - At the oncologist's clinic, I already pictured the pain and agony that would come in the following days. Fear already engulfed me at this time. I was hysterical at this point. I immediately went to my car and cried uncontrollably. I did not know what to do at that time. I was worried about so many things. I did not even know how to tell my husband, my two daughters, my sister, my brothers, and the rest of the family. I asked the Lord God to hug me and let me cry out my pain and agony. I asked the Lord God for the cancer pain to only occur at night when I am home in bed. I did not want to collapse at work, or when driving, or anywhere else. God is faithful. All my pains occurred after seven in the evening, when I am already at home and ready for bed. There was one occurrence in which it started just after I arrived home and opened our back door. I immediately ran to our room and asked my husband to pray over me, anoint me with oil, and change my clothes. God remains faithful all the time.

I also asked the Lord God for forgiveness for my disobedience regarding building a hospital in the Philippines. By March 2014, I already told my sister

Annemarie and my three brothers, regarding the Lord God's mandate. We decided to donate a piece of land that our parents, Alaric and Lydia Acosta, passed down to us five children. My brother Aldric, a medical doctor in the Philippines, started working with his architect friend on the hospital floor plan. They both went to the Department of Health (DOH) in Cagayan de Oro City for review and approval of the hospital plan. I also hired Christy who would be working on the necessary requirements for the land title and conversion and any paperwork for the DOH. I had already informed our church cell group in August about my plan to follow the Lord God's command to build a hospital in the Philippines. I told the Lord God that I would go back to the Philippines one year after the surgery when I was feeling better. But with the situation at that time, feeling better or not, I had already planned to retire from my job and start working on the hospital full time.

Sadness/Depression – Finally, depression set in. I was deeply saddened. I was wondering if I was nearing the end stage of my life. I remembered our church cell leaders, Carmen and Jon, were both knocking at our door one Sunday morning before the eleven o'clock church service. Then Carmen told my husband Joesel and I about her dream. She was ushered by an Asian man into a funeral room. The place was all white. She immediately knew it was me. So they prayed for me. We told them about the Lord God's vision of a hospital in the Philippines. The lung cancer diagnosis had not yet happened at that time. Remembering Carmen's dream made me sad and depressed. Physically, my body was getting weaker. My soul (mind and emotions) was also sad. My spirit was down. I became withdrawn from other people. I constantly talked to the Lord God, my Comforter. I was sad for the bad and wrong decisions or actions I made. I was sad that I did not serve my Lord God well. I was sad that I did not take care of my body that caused the second cancer. I cried a lot. Every time I reflected on the wrong doings in my life, I asked the Lord God for forgiveness that I did not do well in living my life. I asked the Lord God for forgiveness for disobedience and delaying my travel back to the Philippines. I knew I was getting weaker since I had my kidney surgery, but I believed the Lord God would carry me through wherever He leads me. I totally surrendered to His will.

Acceptance -

I asked the Lord God,
"Why two cancers in a year?"
The Lord God responded,
"I want you to tell My people that
I am the Lord God the Healer."

Amazing! The Lord God the Healer's words brought assurance and comfort. That was all I needed to accept everything. Even in my sickness with cancer, God can use me to glorify Himself to tell His people that He is the Lord God the Healer. Hallelujah!

Suddenly, I accepted my fate. I had to rely on the Lord God again and again and again. He fought for all my battles. He will fight all my battles again and again. I knew I have victory in the name of Jesus and by the blood of Jesus and by the words of my testimony. At that point, everything was already a win-win situation for me.

> O death, where is thy sting? O grave, where is thy victory? The sting of death is sin; and the strength of sin is the law. But thanks be to God, which giveth us the victory through our Lord Jesus Christ.
>
> 1 Corinthians 15:55-57, KJV

CHAPTER 5

Victory Over the Second Cancer

The Lord God the Healer was the only One I knew and believed in my heart that would give me victory over cancers. He healed me and rescued me again, and again, and again, over sickness and death throughout my life. He helped me win the battle over the right kidney cancer earlier that year. He would help me win the battle against the metastatic lung cancer that spread to the liver and remaining left kidney. Once again, I had to prepare for another battle, a bigger battle.

Identifying the Enemies - First, I had to identify who my enemies or opponents were, and what were my struggles and difficulties. My enemies were cancers, the sins I committed, and generational curses in my family tree. I also had to identify the list of struggles and difficulties that I would face in the coming days ahead, which included physical, mental, spiritual, medical, insurance, career, financial, family, survivorship, social, and more.

Word of God - Then I had to go back to the Bible, which my pastors referred to as the Basic Instruction Before Leaving Earth (BIBLE). I prayed to the Lord God Almighty, the Author and Finisher of my life, to guide me in the coming days. I told the Lord God that I was ready to face tomorrow. I asked Him to hold my right hand. I stand on His promise in Isaiah 41:13 (KJV): "For I the Lord thy God will hold thy right hand, saying unto thee, Fear not; I will help thee."

Facing my Destiny (Life or Death) - I was extremely excited of the thought that the Lord God. the Author and Finisher of my life, will call me home. I will see the Lord Jesus face-to-face. I will hug Him and walk daily at His side forever. Isn't that the most precious thought of all?

If I will survive, the Lord God the Healer will heal me supernaturally. I told myself to put all my trust in Him. I will go where He wants me to go. I will do whatever He wants me to do. Deuteronomy 28 outlines the blessings for obedience and curses for disobedience to the Lord God Almighty: "The Lord will afflict you with the boils of Egypt and with tumors, festering sores and the itch, from which you cannot be cured" (Deuteronomy 28:27). He said,

> "If you listen carefully to the Lord your God and do what is right in his eyes, if you pay attention to his commands and keep all his decrees, I will not bring on you any of the diseases I brought on the Egyptians, *for I am the Lord, who heals you*" (Exodus 15:26).

Breaking the News and the Preparations - I initially told my husband Joesel about the diagnosis of the probable metastatic lung cancer. I requested him to release the information to anyone else only after Christmas. We wanted to have a festive Christmas season, not one full of sadness and grief. We also didn't want to distract our daughters, Trescha and Selcy, who were having final exams in college. My oldest daughter, Trescha, graduated that December 2014 from the college of nursing. We give the Lord God all the glory, honor, and praise for the blessing. After the Christmas festivities, my husband and I told his family about my medical condition, my retirement from work in February 2015, and my moving to the Philippines to start helping in the planning for the hospital building. I also told my sister and brothers. I told them that I would be in the Philippines at end of March 2015. I gave a notice at the office that my last working day will be February 28, 2015. We called our real estate agent to assist us in preparing the house to be put up on the market. We prepped up the house before selling it on the market. We gave away most of our belongings and furniture to Goodwill and Salvation Army. We are so grateful that, at this time, our family friends since 1992, Monty, Lorna, their son, and their daughter, helped us clean the house and move into an apartment near my husband's place of work. My husband and I also updated both of our living wills. December 2014 to February 2015 were busy preparing for the months ahead.

Cancer Pain - Early November 2014, I noticed that I had difficulty breathing but I thought that this was just due to allergies or the seasonal changes. After I was diagnosed with metastatic lung cancer, by early December 2014 I started having pains in my liver which shot straight up to my head. That scared me big time. Did the cancer spread to my brain that quickly? The previous CT scan only showed metastasis to the liver and kidney. I did not want to know anymore at that time. When the pain started, I needed to be in bed for I could not function anymore after it started. I was totally incapacitated. I cried out to the Lord God asking what to do with the pain. I knew that my sensitive liver and remaining left kidney could not take strong medications. Once I lay down in bed, I called my husband (a cell leader at our church), to anoint my head with oil and pray over me.

> Is anyone among you sick? Let them call the elders of the church to pray over them and anoint them with oil in the name of the Lord. And the prayer offered in faith will make the sick person well; the Lord will raise them up. If they have sinned, they will be forgiven. Therefore confess your sins to each other and pray for each other so that you may be healed. The prayer of a righteous person is powerful and effective.
>
> James 5:14-16

The pains were acute, severe, and lasted from three to five seconds. My pain intensities were severe (mostly 10 or higher) using the 11-point numeric rating scale for pain intensities. In all occasions, the pains started at the liver. It felt like a sharp object, like a saber thrashing and pulling my liver. I felt these intense and acute pains in the liver. Then it moved directly to my brain, passing my chest. The pains were tearing all muscles and nerves near my liver and brain. Then I felt a sharp pain in my heart. The whole ordeal was similar to a super storm but happening inside my body. I remembered Him calming the storm when He and disciples were on a boat.

> That day when evening came, he said to his disciples, "Let us go over to the other side."

> Leaving the crowd behind, they took him along, just as he was, in the boat. There were also other boats with him. A furious squall came up, and the waves broke over the boat, so that it was nearly swamped. Jesus was in the stern, sleeping on a cushion. The disciples woke him and said to him, "Teacher, don't you care if we drown?" He got up, rebuked the wind and said to the waves, "Quiet! Be still!" Then the wind died down and it was completely calm. He said to his disciples, "Why are you so afraid? Do you still have no faith?"
>
> Mark 4:35-40

I always cried out to the Lord Jesus when these storms inside my body came. I said:

"Lord, You are the only One who can calm
down the storms inside my body.
The pain medications are deadly to my liver
and remaining left kidney.
My heart cannot withstand the intensity of
the pain. Remove all my fears.
Increase my faith in You, O Lord. I rebuke
these pains in Your name, Lord Jesus.
By Your precious blood, I am healed and set
free from these pains."

Then the pain stopped. When the pains were gone, I was knocked down to sleep. Then I woke up the next day with renewed energy. It was just like when the Lord Jesus stopped the storm when he was with the disciples on the boat. That was awesome! What a great and mighty God is the Lord God my Healer! The pains were chronic and persistent. The pains came a couple of nights a week over the period of nine months. Every time I called on the name of the Lord God, He repeatedly stopped the pains and storms inside my body. I did not have any pain on my left kidney. I thanked the Lord God for that. I just prayed to the Lord God that when the pain attacked me, I would be at home at night and not anywhere else or even on the road driving. Thank God for that answered prayer all the time.

God's Answer to my Prayers – In February 2015 while we were busy packing for our move, the Lord God spoke to me and said, "Call Gigi."

Immediately, I knew that this was Dr. Siton, who was my classmate since kindergarten in Oroquieta City, Philippines. Dr. Siton, Doctor of Physical Therapy (DPT), was a practicing physical therapist and had her physical therapy clinic in Houston, Texas. I responded to the Lord God that I was busy and did not want to share my current situation with anyone.

Then the Lord God spoke to me the second time and said, "Call Gigi."

I responded to the Lord God, "Lord I am busy with the move and wrapping up my work at USAA before the end of February 2015."

Finally, the Lord God spoke to me the third time: "Call Gigi."

I immediately realized that the Lord God wanted me to listen and follow what He was saying. I asked the Lord God to show me what to talk to Dr. Siton about. I was not sharing my health situation with any other people aside my immediate families. Then I saw Dr. Siton on Facebook reading an epigenetics book. Then I realized I must call Dr. Siton. I told Dr. Siton about my cancer story. She immediately told me to buy the Gerson cancer therapy book. She asked me to go to Houston when the book arrives and stay with her for a couple of weeks, so she can go over the Gerson cancer therapy book with me. I told her that I was scheduled to go to the Philippines before the end of March 2015. I asked if I could visit her after my Philippines trip. She said, "Before you go to the Philippines, stay with me for a couple of weeks to go over the Gerson cancer therapy." I responded, "I can only do five days, from March third through the seventh."

God's Deliverance – God's ways are many, and some are a mystery beyond our simple understanding. We only need to listen and act on His leading to walk on His righteous paths. On March 3, 2015, I drove to Houston from San Antonio, Texas to visit Dr. Siton. That was my first time driving out of town by myself. It was a three-hour drive. My husband Joesel suggested that I drive for an hour then rest in a gas station for a couple of minutes before driving again another hour then rest. I drove for about an hour when I passed by Luling, Texas.

Then the Lord God spoke and said, "Because of your obedience you are healed."
Immediately, I felt a heavy black spirit leaving my body.
I felt refreshed and renewed. To God be the glory for that miracle healing!

God's Healing - I spent the first week after my retirement from USAA in Houston, Texas at Dr. Siton's Holistic Physical Therapy. It felt like going to work in a medical field environment that was totally different from the business environment that I worked in for twenty-five years. It was God's way of preparing me for His commission to build Him a hospital in the Philippines. Dr. Siton has a big heart and was a very hospitable hostess. She let me work on my cancer therapy at her clinic during the day and let me stay at her beautiful home at night. She went over my medical records. She immediately designed therapies for me such as juicing, water therapy, massage therapy, acupuncture, core exercises, coffee enema, sleep, detoxification, and more. I had intensive one-on-one teaching and coaching by Dr. Siton about holistic healing. She let me read books and watch videos about holistic healing. The healings that occurred at Dr. Siton's house were after the first coffee enema. Black tars came out. I felt some release. I did a second coffee enema and felt much better. The massage therapy and core exercises also gave me more strength.

I told Dr. Siton about God's commission to build Him a hospital in the Philippines. During my visit, Dr. Siton showed me hospital designs. She suggested a green hospital which helps in the healing process of the patient. Dr. Siton had a background in engineering before proceeding to physical therapy. She encouraged me and gave me suggestions in building a hospital.

The five-day stay with Dr. Siton was therapeutic and very fruitful. When I was ready to leave, Dr. Siton asked me if the oncologist told me about the cancer stage. I responded that we did not talk about it because I was already scared receiving the news of another cancer in less than a year. I bought a book about lung cancer to learn more about the disease. I knew I was already at the last stage in December 2014 because it metastasized to the liver and remaining left kidney. However, I never mentioned that to any family member. Deep in my heart, I wanted the Lord God to have the last word. Dr.

Siton told me that maybe it would be a two or three, but I knew it was already the end stage. Saying our goodbyes was bittersweet. I thank God that He never gave up on me for prodding me to call Dr. Siton. Visiting Dr. Siton and learning a wealth of knowledge was incredible. I asked the Lord God to forgive me for not taking care of my body. I learned how to remove toxins that plagued our bodies in this modern world. Today, Dr. Siton is sharing her knowledge about holistic healing to thousands of patients around the world.

The First Leg of the Trip – Finally, I was flying out of San Antonio, Texas. My first stop was in Los Angeles, California. I stayed in Winnetka with my loving and hospitable cousins, Didit, husband Jojie, and their two children. Then my other cousin, Winnie, came with her youngest son to pick me up and stay at their home in Solvang, California. We stopped by Santa Barbara for lunch. The beach environment was very therapeutic with its fresh pacific air, soothing sea waves, white sands, and breathtaking views. Then we continued our trip going up to Solvang. The mountain views were refreshing and breathtaking. Finally, we arrived in Solvang. It is a beautiful Danish town. I stayed with my cousin, Winnie, her husband, Chris, and three sons. My cousin Didit and her family came to pick me up in Solvang. We had a wonderful and memorable time together in Solvang. I was very blessed to have the love and support of my cousins in California. It gave me a boost of energy, inspiration, confidence, and hope. God is good all the time. God always put people at the right time and place in my life. To God be the glory!

Trip to the Philippines – Finally, the day came for my trip to the Philippines. My sister, Annemarie, and her husband, Ernesto, picked me up at the airport. Later we met up with my brother, Dr. Aldric G., Sr., his wife, Jennifer, and their son, AJ. We had another wonderful time bonding in Manila before heading back to our hometown in Oroquieta City, Philippines. Our youngest brother picked us up at the airport. Then in April 2015, my brother, Jose, with his wife, Det, and their children, Ella and Josh, arrived from Sydney, Australia. Finally, all five siblings were together to start building the hospital for the Lord God the Healer. Hallelujah!

Upon the Holy Spirit's guidance, we registered the nonprofit hospital as
"Mizmor Kaf Gimmel Hospital."
It is Hebrew for "Psalm of the Good Shepherd" or Psalm 23 (Psalm of David).

Truly, the Lord God the Healer is our Good Shepherd. He is our Provider, Rest, Healer, Refresher of our soul, Guide, Fighter of our battles, Comforter, Protector, Anointer, Lover, and Giver of eternal life. To God be the glory!

The Miraculous Healing Touch of God - As the days passed by, the cancer pain was getting stronger. The cancer pain still knocked me down to sleep in less than five seconds. However, after a couple of months, I noticed that my heart already felt the pain. I remembered feeling like my chest was being cut by a shiny sword that started from my liver then dragged it up to the chest and ended in my head. Night after night, I clung to the Lord God like a baby when the pain started. Morning after morning, I woke up feeling rested, refreshed, and still alive. To God be the glory!

As the months passed, my body was getting weaker. I lost twenty-five pounds. I planned to stay in the Philippines until my next follow-up with the oncologist in June 2015 or after I was healed. By June 2015, the pain in my liver and head continued. I did not want to go back home to San Antonio, Texas without getting a miraculous healing touch by God.

My heart was already burdened after a couple of months of battling the storms within my body. I did not know if I could go on with the physical strength left in me. I felt like a candlestick burning at the last hour. The pain intensities were increasing. The pain frequency became nightly. I told the Lord Jesus how I longed to be in the crowd of people when He was here walking on this earth. The people who were sick and had all kinds of diseases only touched the hem of His garment, and they were made perfectly whole. I stand on the promises of these verses in Matthew:

> And when the men of that place had knowledge of him, they sent out into all that country round about, and *brought unto him all that were diseased*. And *besought him that they might only touch the hem of his garment:* and *as many as touched were made perfectly whole.*
>
> Matthew 14:35-36 (KJV)

I also remembered the woman who was bleeding for twelve years who touched the end of his cloth and immediately the bleeding stopped.

> And, behold, a woman, which was *diseased with an issue of blood twelve years*, came behind him, and *touched the hem of his garment*: For she said within herself, *If I may but touch his garment, I shall be whole.* But Jesus turned him about, and when he saw her, he said, Daughter, be of good comfort; *thy faith hath made thee whole.* And the woman was made whole from that hour.
>
> Matthew 9:20-22 (KJV)

I told the Lord Jesus I remembered His ministry here on earth and how the people with all kinds of diseases were completely healed and made whole.

> Jesus went throughout Galilee, teaching in their synagogues, proclaiming the good news of the kingdom, and healing every disease and sickness among the people. News about Him spread all over Syria, and people brought to Him all who were ill with various diseases, those suffering severe pain, the demon-possessed, those having seizures, and the paralyzed; and He healed them.
>
> Matthew 4:23-24

I told the Lord Jesus I also remembered the people with all kinds of diseases, the blind, the mute, and more. He touched and laid hands on them, and they were all healed. "At sunset, the people brought to Jesus all who had various kinds of sickness, and laying His hands on each one, He healed them" (Luke 4:40).

> As Jesus went on from there, two blind men followed Him, calling out, "Have mercy on us, Son of David!" When He had gone indoors, the blind men came to Him, and He asked them, "Do you believe that I am able to do this?" "Yes,

> Lord," they replied. Then He touched their eyes and said, "According to your faith let it be done to you"; and their sight was restored. Jesus warned them sternly, "See that no one knows about this."
>
> Matthew 9:27-30

One night in July 2015, the pain attacked me again. I was lying down on the bed in my parents' old bedroom at the main house in Oroquieta City. I anointed myself with oil and prayed. I asked the Lord God to deliver me completely from the severe pains.

I cried out to the Lord God Almighty to end my pain and suffering, for my heart could not take it anymore.

"Lord God, take me or heal me. I cannot take
the pain anymore."
Suddenly I saw a light shining as bright as
gold and as bright as the morning sun.
It was the shining hands of the Lord God
reaching out to me.
With my both hands, I reached out for the
hand of the Lord God quickly
and placed it on top of my stomach, near the
liver. Immediately the pain was gone.
What a miracle!

I praised the Lord God for answering my prayers that night. I slept peacefully the whole evening. When I awoke in the morning, I was made brand new. After that night, there were no more pains in my liver, heart, or head. To God be the glory! God is a miracle-working God.

Follow-Up CT Scan Again - In July 2015, I went to the diagnostics center for another CT scan. I was by myself at this time. I remembered the technician asking me after the testing about my medical condition. He mentioned that his grandma also had cancer. I told him simply that I was diagnosed earlier with cancer. He asked what treatments I had, for I looked great. I simply told him that I did not go through chemotherapy, radiation, or any other prescription medications. The Lord God the Healer healed me completely.

Oncologist Follow-Up Again - I was back at my oncologist's clinic a week after the CT scan in early August 2015. My husband Joesel was with me to show support. The wait seemed long this time at the waiting area. Finally, we were called to go to the exam room. We were both waiting with anticipation. The oncologist came into the exam room. He said his short greetings. Then he reviewed my medical records. My heart was already pumping at that time. The oncologist looked at me, then he smiled. He delivered the news saying,

"Your CT scan is beautiful. There is no more trace of cancer."

Hallelujah! Praise the Lord! Truly the Lord God Almighty is the Lord the Healer. I overcame cancer. God fought all my battles with cancer. God gave me the victory over the metastatic lung cancer.

> For everyone born of God is victorious and overcomes the world; and this is the victory that has conquered and overcome the world—our [continuing, persistent] faith [in Jesus the Son of God]. Who is the one who is victorious and overcomes the world? It is the one who believes and recognizes the fact that Jesus is the Son of God.
>
> 1 John 5:4-5 (AMP)

> Concerning this I pleaded with the Lord three times that it might leave me; but He has said to me, "My grace is sufficient for you [My lovingkindness and My mercy are more than enough—always available—regardless of the situation]; for [My] power is being perfected [and is completed and shows itself most effectively] in [your] weakness." Therefore, I will all the more gladly boast in my weaknesses, so that the power of Christ [may completely en-

fold me and] may dwell in me. So, I am well pleased with weaknesses, with insults, with distresses, with persecutions, and with difficulties, for the sake of Christ; for when I am weak [in human strength], then I am strong [truly able, truly powerful, truly drawing from God's strength].

2 Corinthians 12:8-10 (AMP)

Thanksgiving

Praise the Lord God my Healer!
I received from You, my God, Your supernatural and miraculous healing touch.
I am grateful to be embraced by Your eternal love and tender mercies.
Truly Your grace is sufficient in my weakness.
Seeing Your power, O Lord my God, being perfected in my weakness was extraordinary.
You, my God, all powerful (omnipotent).
I was humbled to experience Your power, O Lord, manifested in my life.
I experienced the fullness of joy and the peace that passeth all understanding.
You, O Lord my God, are faithful.
You, O Lord my God,
healed me from two cancers.

Truly You, O Lord my God, healed me again
and again.
Truly You alone are the Lord God the Healer
who healed me completely.
And this is my ministry, to tell Your people
O Lord God that
You are the Lord God the Healer.
Amen.

PART II:

THE HEALING JOURNEY WITH THE LORD GOD MY HEALER

Part II

Part II details the biblical principles that I followed to heal me completely—body, soul, and spirit. The Lord God created mankind as a triune being. We are all created in the image of God. We have a body, soul, and spirit. There is a point in our lives when one part, or two parts, or all three parts become sick. The Lord God is always here for us when we need healing. The Lord God the Healer is the only One who can heal us completely—body, soul, and spirit.

The Lord God desires that we live abundant and healthy lives. He wants us to live our lives to the fullest to achieve our purpose here on earth. We are fearfully and wonderfully made. The Lord God created us with amazing bodies. We need to learn, understand, and practice how to be good stewards of our bodies. This is the Lord God's gift to each one of us.

> For you created my inmost being; you knit me together in my mother's womb.

> I praise you because I am fearfully and wonderfully made; your works are wonderful,
> I know that full well.
>
> Psalm 139:13-14

Call on the name of our Lord God the Healer when we need healing in any areas of our body. Our Lord God the Healer heals all kinds and manners of sicknesses and diseases. There is no distinction between headache and cancer. The Lord God our Healer heals them all. When we draw ourselves near to God, He will draw near to us. When we are in the presence of God, we are complete. Sicknesses and diseases will not come near us. We are under God's protection. He is our Shield. Focus yourself on the Lord God our Healer. Surely, the Lord God our Healer heals you. Surely the Lord God our Healer gives you all the victories in your healing journeys. Praise the Lord! Hallelujah!

Here were the steps that I followed in my healing journey:

1. Ask the Lord God for knowledge, wisdom, and guidance in my healing journey. Ask the Lord God to reveal the areas that needs healing—body, soul, and spirit.
2. Surrender everything to the Lord God. He is the God who is in control of everything.

3. Follow God's guidance. Act on what the Lord God reveals to do. In my healing journey, I told the Lord God that if He asked me to go and dip in the Jordan River like Naaman, I would go to the Jordan River and dip in the water like Naaman.
4. Believe in God. Place trust in God's truth.
5. Put whole faith in God.
6. Do the will of God.
7. Cover with the blood of Jesus. Know the power of the blood of Jesus. "But He was pierced for our transgressions, He was crushed for our iniquities; the punishment that brought us peace was on Him, and by His wounds we are healed" (Isaiah 53:5).
8. Touch God and be healed. The Lord Jesus touched the sick and they were all healed. "And when the men of that place recognized Jesus, they sent word to all the surrounding country. People brought all their sick to Him and begged Him to let the sick just touch the edge of his cloak, and all who touched it were healed" (Matthew 14:35-36). "Jesus reached out his hand and touched the man. 'I am willing,' he said. 'Be clean!' Immediately he was cleansed of his leprosy" (Matthew 8:3). "Jesus had compassion on them and touched their eyes. Immediately they received their sight and followed him" (Matthew 20:34).

9. Wait patiently for the Lord God's healing. Healing is God's will for us. Healing can be instantaneous like the man healed of leprosy (Matthew 8:3), two blind men (Matthew 20:34), a demon-possessed boy (Matthew 17:18), and many more. Healing can also be gradual like the nobleman's sick son (John 4:52-53), ten lepers (Luke 17:12-16), the blind man eyes anointed with clay by Jesus and told to wash in the pool of Siloam (John 9:1-7), and more.
10. Give thanks to God with a grateful heart.
11. Praise the Lord God the Healer. Tune your heart to God.
12. Share the word of your testimony. When we share our testimony, it also gives hope to others who are have the same problems and need to hear the healing power of God to strengthen them.

CHAPTER 6

Meditate on the Word of God

> Blessed is the one who does not walk in step with the wicked or stand in the way that sinners take or sit in the company of mockers, but whose delight is in the law of the Lord, and who meditates on His law day and night. That person is like a tree planted by streams of water, which yields its fruit in season and whose leaf does not wither—whatever they do prospers.
>
> Psalm 1:1-3 (KJV)

The Word of God brings joy, happiness, and great pleasure. It brings delight to our daily living. It inspires us. It moves us. It gives us purpose. And for this very reason, man seeks God and finds Him. When troubles come, such as sickness, sorrow, and even cancer, the Lord God calls me to seek Him with all my heart, mind, body, soul, and spirit.

- Read the Word of God daily.
- Meditate on the Word of God.
- Ask the Lord God for revelation knowledge.
- Ask the Holy Spirit for guidance.

Psalm 1 above was one of my favorite verses since I attended lay ministry training in our hometown church back in 1980. I believe that Christ is the answer to all my troubles and cares. I was devastated about the deadly news of cancer. The first news of the encapsulated right kidney cancer did not alarm me. I saw hope through what my Mommy Lydia went through. She had one kidney removed, and the cancer did not recur until she died in May 2010. Her remaining kidney was healthy. However, hearing about the metastatic lung cancer was deadly and devastating. The people I knew with lung cancer died. The survival rate was low. My liver and remaining left kidney also had some cysts. I initially felt hopeless. I remembered crying in my car after I read the CT scan results. I felt like I was riding in a roller coaster of deadly emotions such as fear, denial, sadness, worry, guilt, shame, overwhelmingness, helplessness, confusion, blame, anger, anxiety, loneliness, and more. I saw and felt this dark spirit that just engulfed my being, and my clock started ticking as if I was near the end of my life. I first denied the diagnosis. Maybe the Diagnostic company made a mistake. This must be someone else's diagnosis, or the machine was broken. But I remembered that I was getting weaker after the kidney surgery. I felt like a candle with only a flicker of light. I finally had the explanation of my weakness, but it was not promising. The spirit of death jumped in once more. How long will I live? Will it be one month, three months, six months, or more? Then the blaming started. What have I done or missed doing? I felt like I was drowning and couldn't breathe.

> This book of the law shall not depart out of thy mouth; but thou shalt meditate therein day and night, that thou mayest observe to do according to all that is written therein: for then thou shalt make thy way prosperous, and then thou shalt have good success.
>
> Joshua 1:8, KJV

I remembered Joshua, who led the Israelites to the Promised Land. I admired Joshua's love, dedication, strength, and courage as he served the Lord God. He trusted and believed in the Lord God Almighty. He saw with his own eyes the Promised Land. He trusted and believed the Lord God to bring them into the Promised Land. Joshua had no fear. He was strong and courageous. Joshua and Caleb were the only two men who were able to go to the Promised Land from those aging twenty and above. All the rest perished in the desert due to disobedience and unbelief in the Lord God, the God of Abraham, Isaac, and Jacob. I saw the Lord God's vision in my life to build Him a hospital in the Philippines. I knew He would see me through to fulfill His vision of building a hospital in the Philippines.

In March 2014, I told my sister and my three brothers of God's vision. We all agreed to donate a piece of land that our parents owned in Mobod, Oroquieta City. My brother Aldric, a medical doctor, already started with the hospital floor plan with his architect friend. I was still in Texas by December 2014. I had already planned to leave my job in February 2015. My husband and I were preparing the house to be sold and already contacted a real estate agent to help us with the process. I asked for forgiveness for the delay in moving to the Philippines to start the hospital. I thought that after six months to a year that my health would be back to normal. But it was the opposite. I was getting weaker. I asked the Lord for strength and courage, physically and spiritually. I believed that the Lord God could make me become strong and courageous to fulfill His vision in my life.

Then I remembered my Lord God, my
Master, my Savior, my Healer, my Redeemer,
and my Friend. The Lord God said,
"Be still. I am in control."

I asked the Lord God, "Why two cancers,
Lord, in less than a year?" And He replied,
"I want you to tell My people that
I am the Lord God the Healer."

I answered "I know that, Lord. I remembered You redeeming me from death and the witch. You healed me from adolescent arthritis. You healed me from ovarian cysts. You stopped the growth of cysts in my breasts. You healed me time and time again. You are the Lord God my Healer. I believe in You. I trust in You. I have no other God beside you." Then I felt a flicker of hope. I knew that the Lord God was in control of my life. It was *"win-win"* for me at that time. I was in a crossroad of my life, where I had to make huge decisions about every aspect of my life. I was overjoyed thinking that I could see the Lord Jesus face-to-face soon. On the other hand, I was also glad that the Lord God my Healer would heal me again, and again, and again. I was humbled that He would use me to show His people that He alone is the Lord God the Healer. I believed that He was Lord God my Creator, and He could heal all my one hundred trillion cells. He can make all my organs brand new. I was grateful that my oncologist only mentioned that word "nodule" instead of "cancer" when I was in the exam room. He also asked me to come back in six months. Those two things definitely gave me a little hope to move to the next steps. I also remembered the healing ministry of the Lord Jesus here on Earth and how He healed every sickness, various disease, severe pain, demon-possession, seizure, leprosy, woman bleeding for twelve years, paralytic, mute, blind person, fever, shriveled hand, and more. The Lord Jesus even brought people back to life, such as Lazarus and the ruler's dead girl. I know that the Lord God breathes life into each of His created beings, including myself. Everything happens in God's perfect time. I had peace meditating on the great and mighty works of the Lord God.

> A new heart also will I give you, and a new spirit will I put within you: and I will take away the stony heart out of your flesh, and I will give you a heart of flesh. And I will put my spirit within you, and cause you to walk in my statutes, and ye shall keep my judgments, and do them. And ye shall dwell in the land that I gave to your fathers; and ye shall be my people, and I will be your God.
>
> Ezekiel 36:26-28 (KJV)

In my meditations, I asked the Lord God to give me a heart of flesh and to remove my heart of stone. The Lord God commissioned me to build a hospital in the Philippines. I knew by faith I need to fulfill His words in my life. I remembered the story of Jonah who was sent by God to prophesy the destruction of Nineveh but tried to escape the divine mission. As the ship sailed out to the sea, a storm came, and the passengers cast a lot to determine who would be thrown overboard. Jonah was chosen and was thrown overboard the ship. A big fish swallowed Jonah. Jonah prayed unto the Lord. And the Lord made the fish vomit Jonah into dry land. Then Jonah followed the command of the Lord to go and preach to Nineveh. Just like Jonah, I need the Lord God to give me another chance. I need the Lord God to lead me, guide me, prepare me, and connect me to the right people. Everything will come to pass in God's perfect time. I prayed that the Lord God open my heart, eyes, and ears to hear His voice (the still small voice), listen to His Words, and diligently follow His commands.

> The purposes of a person's heart are deep waters, but one who has insight draws them out.
>
> Proverbs 20:5

> Put your outdoor work in order and get your fields ready; after that, build your house.
>
> Proverbs 24:27

Forget the former things; do not dwell on the past. See, I am doing a new thing! Now it springs up; do you not perceive it? I am making a way in the wilderness and streams in the wasteland.

Isaiah 43:18-19

CHAPTER 7

Transform/ Renew the Mind

> I beseech you therefore, brethren, by the mercies of God, that ye present your bodies a living sacrifice, holy, acceptable unto God, which is your reasonable service. And be not conformed to this world: but be ye transformed by the renewing of your mind, that ye may prove what is that good, and acceptable, and perfect, will of God.
>
> Romans 12:1-2 (KJV)

Meditating on the Word of God leads to the renewal of the mind. A renewed mind leads to accurate self-talk. I was able to talk to myself based on the Word of God.

- Surrender everything to the Lord God.
- Focus on God's love, mercy, and grace.
- Reject the enemy's lies and deception.
- Believe in God's words and promises.

"But we all, with open face beholding as in a glass the glory of the Lord, are changed into the same image from glory to glory, even as by the Spirit of the Lord" (2 Corinthians 3:18, KJV).

I was reminded of Captain Naaman, a commander of the King of Aram's army, who had leprosy. His Israelite captive maid told him of the Prophet Elisha who lived in Israel. Naaman went to Prophet Elisha. The Prophet Elisha sent a messenger with the message to go and wash in the Jordan River seven times, and the flesh shall come again and he shall be clean. Naaman was initially angry, but later, with the prodding of his servants, went to the Jordan River and dipped seven times. Then his flesh came back again, and he was clean (2 Kings 5).

A couple of months before my cancer diagnosis, a friend approached me and kindly gave a piece of information that she had gathered from several people. They noticed and observed that I had become a "negative person." I was initially shocked. I was at denial at first. But I knew it was true. I asked the Lord for forgiveness. I surrendered everything to the Lord God to transform me and renew my mind.

Joy, a beloved sister in Christ in San Antonio, Texas, gave me a book on March 8, 2015, to encourage me to have a positive thinking in my healing journey. The book was written by Dr. Caroline Leaf, entitled *Who Switched Off My Brain?: Controlling Toxic Thoughts and Emotions.*

Dr. Leaf said, "A thought may seem harmless, but if it becomes toxic, it can become physically, emotionally or spiritually dangerous."[1] She further said that "every time you have a thought, it is actively changing your brain and your body—for better or for worse."[2] In her book, she said, "You really can overcome toxic thinking and its effects. You really can renew and refresh the mind. Not only does Scripture uphold this principle, but science proves that when we work with how our brains are wired, lasting, life-giving change is really possible."[3]

The kidney cancer pain started about four years before the kidney cancer surgery. After both my parents, Papa Alaric and Mommy Lydia, died three months apart in 2010, I was overwhelmed by grief. It lasted for about two years. I remembered the Lord telling me, "End your grieving over the death of your parents." I was very glad that that season of grieving ended.

Then another season started. My family had three car accidents in 2012. My husband hit a tire on the Texas highway that caused major damage to our daughter Trescha's car. Thank God there were no physical injuries to my husband Joesel and my daughter Trescha. The car was fixed in a week. Then a week later, Trescha was involved in another accident with the same newly fixed car, trying to avoid a tire on the highway. The car flew to the top of the IH-10 and Loop 1604 interchange in San Antonio, Texas and landed at the bottom near a creek.

The car was totally damaged. Trescha walked away from the accident with no major injuries, and no other car nor person was involved in the accident. Minutes before the accident, the Holy Spirit prompted me to pray. *I just prayed, "Help."* Thank God for the protection and preserving Trescha's life. Then in November 2012, I was hit by another car as I tried to change lanes inside the University of Texas in San Antonio private road. Thank God we were both okay. However, a couple of weeks later the insurance called that the other party claimed bodily injury. I was shocked, and fear engulfed me. My boss, Lorie, calmed me down by assuring me to let the USAA insurance team take care of the accident issues. Accidents happen, but life still has to go on.

I was crippled by fear of the vehicular accidents in 2012. I was afraid of vehicular accidents that I saw on the Texas highways, to the point that I don't want to drive anymore. I finally even carpooled with my husband Joesel to work. Since my husband's work schedule was early, I had to change my work schedule too. It only lasted a couple of weeks, for I am not an early riser.

In November 2012, my husband also had a major heart attack. The whole experienced shook me to the point of almost breaking me down.

In Dr. Leaf's book, *Who Switched Off My Brain*, she said, "Thoughts are basically electrical impulses, chemicals and neurons. They look like a tree with branches.

As the thoughts grow and become permanent, more branches grow and the connections become stronger. As we change our thinking, some branches go away, new ones form, the strength of the connections change, and the memories network with other thoughts. What an incredible capacity of the brain to change and rewire and grow! Spiritually, this is renewing the mind."[4]

Dr. Siton showed me also some books and pictures online on how our thoughts (negative and positive) are like trees with branches that can affect our health and can even make us sick. "We demolish arguments and every pretension that sets itself up against the knowledge of God, and we take captive every thought to make it obedient to Christ" (2 Corinthians 10:5).

I knew I had to make major changes in my thought process. I had to eliminate all the negative thinking and all the sinful emotions such as fear, grief, doubt, unbelief, anger, and more.

- Read the Scripture (Bible, Word of God).
- Spend time in prayer.
- Listen to the voice of God.
- Serve God.

I knew that I needed to be patient on God's plan for my life and my healing process. I had to dismiss all doubts, unbelief, fear, anxiety, and all other negative thoughts that came with the sickness. For my healing, I would have loved an instant miracle. As a child, I experienced His instant miracles and grace on my life as He saved me from the witch and death. I knew the Lord God would heal me in His own perfect time. I was very excited and full of hope. As I did my research and read books on cancer healing, several doctors recognized and mentioned that there was no medication to heal cancer, but they refer you to look up to your Source (that's God) for healing. This gave me great hope. I was on the right track. For I know that my Lord my God is the Lord God the Healer. As I meditate on the Word of God, the Holy Spirit was teaching me to learn about my body (how to feed my body, how to connect to my Source of Healing, the Lord God Almighty), and the Lord God would do all the rest of the healing and restoration. After my kidney surgery, I attended seminars, read books, and watched online or on the television any topics regarding health, wellness, and healing. I realized I had a lot to learn and cover, since my educational and work background were more on the financial and accounting. I learned that our bodies do not know the diseases and illnesses we bear. The body will not recognize if it has a headache, cancer, cough, cold, fever, or any other disease or illness. The body will only know if it is in "fight-or-flight" response. This is a physiological reaction that occurs in response to a perceived harmful event, attack, or threat to survival. Learning about this new information gave me great hope. The Lord God always assured me that "I am the Lord God the Healer. I want my people to know that I am still the Lord God the Healer." I acknowledged the Lord God that He is my Healer. I believed it in my heart.

> Finally, brothers and sisters, whatever is true, whatever is noble, whatever is right, whatever is pure, whatever is lovely, whatever is admirable—if anything is excellent or praiseworthy—think about such things. Whatever you have learned or received or heard from me, or seen in me—put it into practice. And the God of peace will be with you.
>
> Philippians 4:8-9

CHAPTER 8

Speak the Word of God

And God said, "Let there be light," and there was light...And God said, "Let there be a vault between the waters to separate water from water." So God made the vault and separated the water under the vault from the water above it. And it was so...And God said, "Let the water under the sky be gathered to one place, and let dry ground appear." And it was so...And God said, "Let there be lights in the vault of the sky to separate the day from the night, and let them serve as signs to mark sacred times, and days and years, and let them be lights in the vault of the sky to give light on the earth." And it was so...And God said, "Let the land produce living creatures according to their kinds: the livestock, the creatures that move along the ground, and the wild animals, each according to its kind." And it was so.

Genesis 1:3, 6-7, 9, 14-15, 24

I learned about God's creation when I was a little child in Sunday school class. God said, "...and there was...and it was so." Wow! It was powerful!

- Have faith in God.
- Believe in your heart.
- Stop doubting.
- Speak out loud the Word of God.

"Consequently, faith comes from hearing the message, and the message is heard through the word about Christ" (Romans 10:17). "For verily I say unto you, That whosoever shall say unto this mountain, Be thou removed, and be thou cast into the sea; and shall not doubt in his heart, but shall believe that those things which he saith shall come to pass; he shall have whatsoever he saith" (Mark 11:23, KJV).

God wants us to exercise the power of the Word. We *say, speak, declare the Word of God,* and it will manifest and come into being. As a little child, I had a learning disability. I was slow in my learning growth. I spoke when I was almost two years old. My older sister, Annemarie, spoke when she was less than a year old. When I received the Lord Jesus as my Lord and Savior, He healed me miraculously from a deadly fever. In the days following, I asked Him to heal my head, that it would not have any effects of the high fever and seizures that I had experienced all the time during my childhood, until I was healed. I also asked the Lord God to give me knowledge and wisdom to help me excel in school. I also asked the Lord God that I would not get sick anymore so I would not miss any school days. Hallelujah! God is good. He answered all my prayers by the end of second grade. My grades were better in the third grade. I was in the top ten percent of the class. Wow! What an awesome answered prayer. I am just amazed how the big God can hear from and listen to a small child. I was ecstatic when God answers my prayer. It was sometimes an indescribably beautiful feeling. Attending Sunday school most of my childhood, and then joining Bible studies in my teens and adulthood, led me to understand and know the Lord God in a very personal and intimate way. I am just amazed of the great and mighty things that He can do for me. Truly my faith increases. "The Spirit gives life; the flesh counts for nothing. The words I have spoken to you—they are full of the Spirit and life" (John 6:63).

As I was battling with cancer, I came closer to the Lord in prayer. I was at the point that I did not even listen to anyone. I only believed and listened to the Lord God. All my doubts were gone. I remembered the power of the Word.

I also had faith that, when I spoke the Word of God over the one hundred trillion cells of my body (especially those in the liver, kidney, lungs, heart, and head), they would be all healed in the mighty name of Jesus, the power of the precious blood of Jesus, and the power of my testimony.

I also knew of the power of declaration of the Word so that it would manifest in my life. I spoke life into my sick body. I spoke the Bible verses into my life. I believed when I spoke that the words would come to pass. I no longer doubt. The Lord God is my only hope. I spoke healing of the one hundred trillion cells in my body. I spoke healing over my liver; I spoke healing over my kidney. I spoke healing over my heart; I spoke healing over my head.

"Lord, I believe You are
the Lord God my Healer.
You heal all one hundred trillion
cells of my body.
You heal all my organs—lungs, liver,
remaining left kidney, and heart.
You heal my body, my mind,
my emotions, and my spirit.
You are the God who will
make me whole again.
By Jesus' stripes, I am healed.
In the name of Jesus, I am healed."

I kept reading the Bible day and night. I asked the Holy Spirit to guide me and direct me to those Bible verses that speak the truth and life into my sick body. "My mouth will speak words of wisdom; the meditation of my heart will give you understanding" (Psalm 49:3). "This is what we speak, not in words taught us by human wisdom but in words taught by the Spirit, explaining spiritual realities with Spirit-taught words" (1 Corinthians 2:13). "If anyone speaks, they should do so as one who speaks the very words of God. If anyone serves, they should do so with the strength God provides, so that in all things God may be praised through Jesus Christ. To him be the glory and the power for ever and ever. Amen" (1 Peter 4:11).

When we seek the Holy Spirit, He will teach us how to speak. He will tell us what to declare. Just believe. Even when I grew weaker, I spoke boldly just like when the Spirit of the Lord told Ezekiel to speak over the dead bones, and they became alive.

> The hand of the Lord was on me, and He brought me out by the Spirit of the Lord and set me in the middle of a valley; it was full of bones. He led me back and forth among them, and I saw a great many bones on the floor of the valley, bones that were very dry. He asked me, "Son of man, can these bones live?" I

said, "Sovereign Lord, you alone know." Then he said to me, "Prophesy to these bones and say to them, 'Dry bones, hear the word of the Lord! This is what the Sovereign Lord says to these bones: I will make breath enter you, and you will come to life. I will attach tendons to you and make flesh come upon you and cover you with skin; I will put breath in you, and you will come to life. Then you will know that I am the Lord.'"

Ezekiel 37:1-6

CHAPTER 9

Forgive and Forget

> Search me, O God, and know my heart: try me, and know my thoughts: And see if there be any wicked way in me, and lead me in the way everlasting.
>
> Psalm 139:23-24 (KJV)

I learned from reading the Bible and on my faith in the Lord God that those sicknesses and diseases can be attributed to a sin or sins. I was overwhelmed with guilt and shame. I was afraid of the result of the deadly disease. I was greatly affected by the criticism and judgment I would receive from family, friends, healthcare providers, people at church, and others. I asked the Lord God to search my entire being and see any wicked ways in me, forgive me of all my sins, and lead me in the way everlasting. My only desire is to be with the Lord Jesus Christ in Heaven forever and ever without end.

- Acknowledge sins.
- Confess sins to God.

- Ask forgiveness from God.
- Receive forgiveness from God.

What Was Going on Inside My Body – In February 2014, I was diagnosed with kidney cancer. The lungs were clean. However, nine months later a nodule was found on the right lung. Since I did not get the detailed explanation of my diagnosis, I researched more about lung cancer to help me understand the disease. I read the book *Lung Cancer: Myths, Facts, Choices—and Hope.* The book said that "each type of cancer has its own staging system, but they're all based on the same three factors: the size and invasiveness of the tumor, lymph node involvement, and spread to other parts of the body (metastasis)."[5] It helped me figure out the stage of the cancer since I didn't ask my oncologist about the stage due to fear. At this point, I was ready to face the reality. I finally accepted that the cancer was at the last stage (stage IV), for it already metastasized to the other organs, such as the liver and remaining left kidney. However, I was glad that it didn't affect the lymph nodes. The book also discussed about how to live with lung cancer especially optimizing the quality of life and hope. The reality was devastating. But the hope that I found in the Lord was promising. I was prepared to face the cancer battle.

> So Moses chiseled out two stone tablets like the first ones and went up Mount Sinai early in the morning, as the Lord had commanded him; and he carried the two stone tablets in his hands. Then the Lord came down in the cloud and stood there with him and proclaimed his name, the Lord. And he passed in front of Moses, proclaiming, "The Lord, the Lord, the compassionate and gracious God, slow to anger, abounding in love and faithfulness, maintaining love to thousands, and forgiving wickedness, rebellion and sin. Yet he does not leave the guilty unpunished; *he punishes the children and their children for the sin of the parents to the third and fourth generation.*"
>
> Exodus 34:4-7

Genetics was a huge part of the diseases that plagued my body. The Bible mentions about generational curses that are passed on to the third and fourth generations. We learned in church how to break generational curses. I thought all my generational curses were already broken down. Read the book by Derek Prince, *Blessing or Curse: You Can Choose.* My mother had kidney cancer when she was sixty years old. One of her kidneys was removed. I contracted the disease when I was forty-eight years old. My right kidney was removed. As a child growing up in the Philippines, lung diseases were prevalent. I was diagnosed as a child with primary complex. Our parents were careful to provide a healthy living environment for us at home. Smoking was not allowed. When I was a teenager, I was diagnosed with adolescent arthritis. There was no cure, but there were pain killers to help manage the pain. The doctor advised against drinking alcohol, smoking, and taking drugs. Growing up, I was very careful not to abuse drugs or prescription medications. I only took medications unless it was necessary to treat a particular disease and only for a short period of time. Every time I got sick, I asked my parents where I got it. Was it hereditary? I learned that my father also had a weak lung, and arthritis ran in his family. My mother's family, on the other hand, had a history with asthma. As an adult, I developed some allergies when I started working in the big city of Manila, Philippines in 1987. But this went away when I moved to Ramstein, Germany with my husband in 1992. In 1995, I was treated for a positive tuberculosis skin test. The treatment was stopped, for it affected my liver and I did not develop the disease. We moved to San Antonio, Texas in 1998, and after a few years, I again developed allergies. I took some prescription or over-the-counter medications on and off. Difficulty in breathing was an occasional problem in my adult life in San Antonio. I never regained my energy back after my surgery to remove my right kidney in February 2014. I was tired most of the time.

> "In your anger do not sin': Do not let the sun go down while you are still angry, and do not give the devil a foothold.
>
> Ephesians 4:26-27

I also had some emotional burdens that I carried for a long time. Both my parents died in 2010. My father died in February 2010. My mother died in May 2010. As I observed my parents' health struggles in their last years that eventually led to their deaths, I was filled with grief, sadness, and inner crying. Early in 2012, I heard the Lord say that I should end my mourning. I realized that I needed to turn my mourning into dancing. Then in November 2012, my husband Joesel had a major heart attack and congested heart failure. I again went into grief, sadness, inner crying, and depression. There were areas in my life that my expectations were not achieved and that totally spiraled down my mental and emotional health.

> If we confess our sins, he is faithful and just to forgive us our sins, and to cleanse us from all unrighteousness.
>
> 1 John 1:9, KJV

My parents instilled in my mind to always seek the Lord God our Creator, who can heal our sick bodies.

It was imperative to go to church every week, for the church was like a hospital for the sin-sick soul, as my parents taught me when I was a child. We did not have any health insurance growing up. But thank God that every time we got sick, the Lord God our Healer also healed us all the time. I asked the Lord God the Father to forgive me of all my sins that I knew, sins that I did not know, and to cleanse me of all my unrighteousness. I asked the Lord Jesus Christ to cleanse me with His precious blood and make me white as snow.

> For God so loved the world, that he gave his only begotten Son, that whosoever believeth in him should not perish, but have everlasting life.
>
> John 3:16, KJV

This is my favorite verse of the Bible. I genuinely felt the love of the Lord God when I was first saved from death and the witch. I believed that the Lord God gave His only begotten Son to die for us on the cross in Calvary. And if we only believed, we would not perish but have everlasting life. This Bible verse came into being in my life and I was amazed of the power of the name of the Lord Jesus Christ and His precious blood.

> Do not be afraid. I am the First and the Last. I am the Living One; I was dead, and now look,

I am alive for ever and ever! And I hold the keys of death and Hades".

Revelations 1:17b-18

Hallelujah! The Lord Jesus Christ proclaimed that He is the First and the Last, He is the Living One. He died, and now He is alive for ever and ever. He holds the keys of death and Hades. This verse will always be comforting and will always increase my faith and confidence in the Lord Jesus Christ. I have all my faith and trust in the Lord Jesus. I have victory in the name of the Lord Jesus Christ!

CHAPTER 10

Prayer and Fasting

> This, then, is how you should pray: "Our Father in heaven, hallowed be your name, your kingdom come, your will be done, on earth as it is in heaven. Give us today our daily bread. And forgive us our debts, as we also have forgiven our debtors. And lead us not into temptation but deliver us from the evil one."
>
> Matthew 6:9-13

Prayer - Prayer is how the people talk to God. Prayer is one of the most powerful weapons God has given us. Through the years after I received the Lord Jesus as my Savior and Lord, I noticed that I talk to Him like I talk to my earthly Papa Alaric: a simple conversation. During my prayer conversation, I praise Him, thank Him, ask Him for anything, cry out to Him, seek guidance, share my thoughts and feelings, and more. He is my Abba Father, the Lord Jesus my Savior and Friend, and the Holy Spirit my Guide.

- Address God.
- Praise God.
- Thank God.
- Ask God.

Pray continually, in the morning, in the evening, and at noon. Pray even if the Holy Spirit wakes you up at three in the morning. Pray anywhere and everywhere the Lord God asks you. Pray in your room, at home, at work, in the field, at church, in your car, in the sea, and anywhere else.

> Pray continually, give thanks in all circumstances; for this is God's will for you in Christ Jesus.
>
> 1 Thessalonians 5:17-18

Pray individually as the Holy Spirit leads you. The Lord asks His disciples to devote themselves in prayer. Pray collectively with your family, friends, church, or any group of people. Join prayer groups in church, at work, in the community, or online. Organize prayer groups if you cannot find any in your area. Organize prayer groups for men, women, youth, senior citizens, or any kind of group. Pray together in person or pray together online (e.g., Zoom meeting, Facebook Messenger Groups, etc.). Jesus promised that He would be in our midst when we gather together in His name. And the Lord Jesus also promised that He would do whatever we ask Him in prayer.

> For where two or three gather in my name, there am I with them.
>
> Matthew 18:20

> And I will do whatever you ask in my name, so that the Father may be glorified in the Son.
>
> John 14:13

> Do not be anxious about anything, but in every situation, by prayer and petition, with thanksgiving, present your requests to God. And the peace of God, which transcends all understanding, will guard your hearts and your minds in Christ Jesus.
>
> Philippians 4:6-7

> This is the confidence we have in approaching God: that if we ask anything according to his will, he hears us.
>
> 1 John 5:14

> Therefore I tell you, whatever you ask for in prayer, believe that you have received it, and it will be yours.
>
> Mark 11:24

> And when He was come into the house, His disciples asked Him privately, Why could not we cast him out? And He said unto them, This kind can come forth by nothing, but by *prayer and fasting*.
>
> Mark 9:28-29, KJV

Being a cancer patient, I knew that I must get rid of a lot of toxins. I had to cleanse both my body and soul. Thus, I made a commitment to choose this path. I surrendered and submitted everything to the Lord God my Healer. I asked the Lord God to humble me and give me strength to follow Him in my healing journey, for He alone can heal me completely.

> Then Esther sent this reply to Mordecai: "Go, gather together all the Jews who are in Susa, and fast for me. Do not eat or drink for three days, night or day. I and my attendants will fast as you do. When this is done, I will go to the king, even though it is against the law. And if I perish, I perish."
>
> Esther 4:15-16

The Bible teaches us about fasting. Men and women both in the Old and New Testaments followed it. Some did it publicly, and others did it privately. There was always a specific purpose for their fast. The Spirit of the Lord moved to answer the purpose of their fast, such as deliverance from their enemies, healing, and more. The length of the fast is dependent on God's guidance: one day, three days, three weeks, one month, forty days, etc.

> At that time I, Daniel, mourned for three weeks. I ate no choice food; no meat or wine touched my lips; and I used no lotions at all until the three weeks were over.
>
> Daniel 10:2-3

As I was deciding on the biblical fast, I asked the Lord God for guidance. The Gerson cancer therapy book already limited my food intake to juicing (e.g., carrots, green apple, greens, beetroot, etc.); no meat, fish, or fowl; no processed foods, no sugar, no carbohydrates, and more. By March 2015, I was getting weak, and my appetite was getting low. By prompting of the Holy Spirit, I decided to follow the juice fast and not eat any meat, carbohydrates (especially rice and bread), sugar, etc. The purpose of the fast was healing from cancer and pain. I was living in Oroquieta City, Philippines at our parents' house at this time. My sister Annemarie even hired an assistant to help me with the juicing and all my other needs. I was able to focus on the Lord. The length of the fast was undetermined. I would not stop until I received my complete healing from cancer and pain from the Lord God my Healer. Praise the Lord for giving me the strength to do the fasting.

> "Even now," declares the Lord, "return to me with all your heart, with fasting and weeping and mourning."
>
> Joel 2:12

As the days turned to a week, the week turned to a month, then two months, then three months. I remember weeping and mourning most days and nights. I remember that this was also the most beautiful time in my life, communing with the Lord God. I was drawn closer and deeper to my Creator, Lord, and Savior. I spent these times in adoration, confession, thanksgiving, supplication, listening, worshiping, praising, and reading the Bible.

I believe in the power of fasting. It draws you nearer to God. It is a time that you are focused on God alone. Hallelujah!

> While they were worshiping the Lord and fasting, the Holy Spirit said, "Set apart for me Barnabas and Saul for the work to which I have called them."
>
> Acts 13:2

The Lord God set me apart to serve Him, to build a hospital for Him in the Philippines. It was a humbling experience to be called by the most high God to serve Him here on Earth. To God be the glory!

CHAPTER 11

Breath of Life

> And the Lord God formed man of the dust of the ground, and breathed into his nostrils the breath of life; and man became a living soul.
>
> Genesis 2:7 (KJV)

The Bible tells us that the Lord God is the air that man breathes. All human beings' lives depend on the Lord God the Creator and Maker of all things. Our Lord God created our human bodies with complexity and uniqueness. Our bodies speak volumes about the mind of our Creator.

> The Spirit of God has made me; the breath of the Almighty gives me life.
>
> Job 33:4

Being diagnosed with cancer, especially one that affected my right lung, made me anxious and nervous. When my physical body failed, I was out of breath sometimes. Then I always reminded myself of the Spirit of God that is within me, who gives me life. This verse is very powerful. My belief in the Spirit of God, my Breath of Life kept me going strong each day. I was living each breath, each second, with the breath of the Almighty God. What a beautiful promise that I hold dearly with each breath I take!

> But it is the spirit in a person, the breath of the Almighty, that gives them understanding.
>
> Job 32:8

I wanted to understand what was going inside my body with all the different cysts growing inside me that resulted in surgeries, even cancer. I was a financial businessperson and knew little about my body systems. I wanted to learn more and understand better to help me take care of myself better. I knew my life was God's gift to me, that I was responsible to take care of it each day. I knew God left us instructions through the Bible (Basic Instruction Before Leaving Earth). My hunger for more knowledge increased. When I was sick, my intellectual ability decreased also. But I know the Lord God Almighty, our good Teacher who gives us knowledge, wisdom, counsel, and understanding. I called upon Him and asked Him to be my Teacher and Guide. I read the Bible back and forth, specifically reading the stories of faith and miraculous healing. I read also books about cancer, specifically lung, kidney, and liver. I searched the Internet for people who shared their experiences, pains, sorrows, and victories. God is good all the time. I thanked God that His Divine Spirit opened the spirit of man within me to help me understand about my body and how to take care of myself.

How We Breathe - Air (oxygen) is the first basic need that the man needs to survive. Man can only live three minutes without air. Approximately one pint of air enters into the body each time a person inhales. The same amount of air leaves the body a few seconds later. In this brief time, the respiratory system moves the oxygen into the blood streams and extracts carbon dioxide. The respiratory system includes the nose, pharynx, larynx, trachea, bronchi, alveoli, and lungs. A healthy lung contains more than three hundred million alveoli. The heart pumps blood through the body via a network of blood vessels. Oxygen-rich blood leaves the lungs and flows to the heart, which pumps it to the rest of the body. Oxygen is needed for our one hundred trillion cells to live and function properly. Carbon Dioxide is a waste product of cellular function. Disposing of this waste is as important as providing oxygen.

What Protects the Lungs - The respiratory system has a defense mechanism that involves cilia, which filters the particles and pathogens that pass through, and triggers a cough when necessary. The second defense mechanism is the lymphatic (immune) system which guards against infection and disease. The lymph, a fluid rich in different types of white blood cells (leukocytes), bathes all the tissues of the body including the lungs. The white blood cells are an army against infection and disease, including cancer.

When Defenses Break Down - The Lord God our Creator created and designed the respiratory system to guard against occasional invaders. These invaders can come from the environment (smoking, chemicals, air pollution), genetics, and lung diseases. However, exposure to irritants can make the natural defenses inadequate or counterproductive. Negative emotions (e.g., sadness, grief, inner crying, anxiety, depression, etc.) can affect the function of the lungs and the whole respiratory system that can eventually lead to diseases and illnesses.

How Long Can Man Live without Air - The human body can only live three minutes without air. Permanent brain damage occurs after four minutes. Death can occur four to six minutes later. Mankind depends on the Lord God. He is the Author and Finisher of our lives.

In his hand is the life of every creature and the breath of all mankind.

Job 12:10

When you hide your face, they are terrified; when you take away their breath, they die and return to the dust.

Psalm 104:29

This is what the Sovereign Lord says to these bones: I will make breath enter you, and you will come to life...I looked, and tendons and flesh appeared on them and skin covered them, but there was no breath in them. Then he said to me, "Prophesy to the breath; prophesy, son of man, and say to it, 'This is what the Sovereign Lord says: Come, breath, from the four winds and breathe into these slain, that they may live.'" *So I prophesied as he commanded me, and breath entered them*; they came to life and stood up on their feet—a vast army.

Ezekiel 37:5, 8-10

This is what God the Lord says—the Creator of the heavens, who stretches them out, who spreads out the earth with all that springs from it, *who gives breath to its people*, and life to

> those who walk on it: "I, the Lord, have called you in righteousness; I will take hold of your hand. I will keep you and will make you to be a covenant for the people and a light for the Gentiles, to open eyes that are blind, to free captives from prison and to release from the dungeon those who sit in darkness.
>
> Isaiah 42:5-7

Taking Care of the Air We Breathe - Trust in the Lord God our Creator, the Spirit of God who is the Breath of Life. Acknowledge Him daily and thank Him for each precious living breath. Clear the lungs and its passageways not only of physical debris, but also negative emotions which become sins that affect our overall health. God is a miracle-working God. He will do miracles again and again. What a loving and beautiful God we have.

> Again Jesus said, "Peace be with you! As the Father has sent me, I am sending you." And with that he breathed on them and said, "Receive the Holy Spirit."
>
> John 20:21-22

CHAPTER 12

Living Water

> Jesus answered, "Everyone who drinks this water will be thirsty again, but whoever drinks the water I give them will never thirst. Indeed, the water I give them will become in them a spring of water welling up to eternal life."
>
> John 4:13-14

The Bible tells us that when we are thirsty, the Lord God will give us living water that will become a spring of water welling up to eternal life, and rivers of living water that will flow from within. Life cannot exist without water. All living things, plants and animals, need water. All human beings need water to survive. God gives us water by sending rain that will go to the rivers. God also gives us water flowing from natural springs. We need to acknowledge and recognize our Creator and Maker of heaven and Earth that we continually depend on; we need Him for our daily provisions of living water for our survival.

> On the last and greatest day of the festival, Jesus stood and said in a loud voice, "Let anyone who is thirsty come to me and drink. Whoever believes in me, as Scripture has said, rivers of living water will flow from within them."
>
> John 7:37-38

How the Body Uses Water - The human body is composed of sixty to eighty percent water. The brain is composed of seventy-five percent water. The bones are composed of twenty-two percent water. The muscles are composed of seventy-five percent of water. The blood is composed of ninety-two percent of water. Water has different functions for the body. It carries nutrients and oxygen to the cells. It helps regulate body temperature. It aids in digestion and prevents constipation. It moistens tissues such as those in the mouth, eyes, and nose. It protects the body's tissue, spinal cord, and organs and lubricates the joints. It lessens the burden of the kidneys and liver by flushing out waste products. It helps dissolve minerals and other nutrients to make them accessible to the body.

When the Body Loses Water - The body loses water through breathing, sweating, and digestion. Thus, it is important to rehydrate by drinking fluids or eating foods that contain water. When the body loses too much fluid through diarrhea, vomiting, and sweating or not drinking water, then dehydration occurs. The body can go into shock which can be life threatening.

How Much Water Does the Body Need - Growing up, we heard the rule to drink eight eight-ounce glasses of water a day. We also heard that another rule for estimating adequate daily water intake is to drink half your total body weight in ounces. For example, if you weigh one hundred and forty pounds, you need to drink seventy fluid ounces daily. The Institute of Medicine determined that an adequate intake (AI) for men is roughly about thirteen cups (three liters) of total beverages a day.[6] The AI for women is about nine cups (two liters and two fluid ounces) of total beverages a day.[7] One needs to modify the total water intake depending on their activity, climate, and health status.

How Long Can Man Live without Water - Man can live without water for three to four days. We've heard on the news how people, young and old, die of dehydration, especially in an extreme hot weather conditions in just a few hours. We need water for our body to function properly. Hydrate with water, other beverages, and fruits and vegetables which are high in water content such as cucumber, watermelon, cantaloupe, lettuce, cabbage, and more.

CHAPTER 13

Bread of Life

> Jesus answered, "It is written: Man shall not live on bread alone, but on every word that comes from the mouth of God."
>
> Matthew 4:4

Spiritual Food - Man must rely on the Lord God for spiritual feeding through the Word of God. The Word of God can be found in the Bible. We need to read this every day to feed our soul and spirit. Get a Bible (with the version of your choice) or you can get it online (e.g., Bible Gateway, Bible Hub, etc.).

I read the King James Version (KJV), New International Version (NIV), New American Standard Bible (NASB), and the Amplified Bible (AMP) in the English language. On some years, I read from Genesis to Revelation or New Testament then Old Testament, or I read a few chapters of both Old and New Testaments, or I followed a daily devotion on any book of the Bible, etc. Ask the Holy Spirit for guidance. He will lead you.

> Then Jesus declared, "*I am the bread of life.* Whoever comes to me will never go hungry, and whoever believes in me will never be thirsty."
>
> John 6:35

> *I am the living bread* that came down from heaven. Whoever eats this bread will live forever. This bread is my flesh, which I will give for the life of the world.
>
> John 6:51

In the book of John, the Lord Jesus Christ fed the five thousand people out of five small barley loaves and two small fish. The people began saying that "surely this is the Prophet who is to come into the world" and they intended to make Him king by force (John 6:14). So the Lord Jesus Christ withdrew to a mountain by Himself. When the people saw him later on the other side of the lake, the Lord Jesus Christ told them that they were looking for Him not because they saw the signs that He performed, but because they ate the loaves and had their fill. Then the Lord Jesus Christ told them, "I am the bread of life...I am the living bread that came down from heaven" (John 6:48, 51).

When I was sick, my body, soul, and spirit were also weak. There was a deep hunger and desire in my being to search the Lord God in a higher and deeper way from every corner of the world. I knew and believed that when I went to the Lord Jesus, He would never drive me away; He would not lose me but raise me up at the last day. I asked the Lord Jesus Christ to give me the bread of life, for I believed that only this bread could give me strength to survive each day. Truly, He was my daily bread. His words fed my soul and spirit each day and sustained me.

Physical Food - A human being can survive for twenty-one days to forty days without food, and then they perish. To survive, our body needs the proper nutrients such as protein, carbohydrates (e.g., bread, etc.), vitamins, and minerals. The twelve body systems need all the proper nutrients to perform their different functions. For example, the digestive system needs vitamin A, vitamin B, vitamin C, vitamin D, magnesium, calcium, healthy fats, fiber–rich and low starch foods. The cardiovascular system needs omega-3 fatty acids, quercetin, folate, coenzyme Q10 (CoQ10), monounsaturated fats, L-carnitine, lycopene, magnesium, and resveratrol.

I inquired the Lord God to give me knowledge and wisdom on how to feed my body. I knew when I was a child there were several foods that my body did not take well. However, through the years I had overcome this and was eating mostly all kinds of food. My food choices were not healthy. I read the Bible for guidance. In Genesis 2:9, the Lord God made all kinds of trees grow from the soil; every tree was pleasing to look at and good for food. Now the tree of life and the tree of the knowledge of good and evil were in the middle of the orchard. The Lord God commanded Adam and Eve, "You are free to eat from any tree in the garden; but you must not eat from the tree of the knowledge of good and evil, for when you eat from it you will certainly die" (Genesis 16b-17). Adam and Eve were mostly feasting on the fruits and vegetables. In Leviticus and Deuteronomy, the Israelites were required to eat clean meat (certain parts of the animal only, but not the fat and blood) from certain types of animals (e.g., lamb, goat, etc.). The Prophet Daniel and his friends ate vegetables and drank water for ten days so the guard could compare them with the young men who ate the royal food and wine. After ten days, the guard found them to look healthier and better nourished. The Lord Jesus Christ ate bread, fish, and lamb (for the Passover meal) as recorded in the Bible. However, people back in the Lord Jesus' time ate mostly plant-based, clean diets such as lentils, whole grains, fruits, vegetables, nuts, and fish. The Lord God designed our bodies to eat certain kinds of foods that give us nutrients and sustain our bodies. However, the food chain in our time is loaded with toxic chemicals, genetically modified organisms (GMOs), processed foods, and more. Eating these types of foods could lead to a myriad of diseases and illnesses.

My Food Protocol - I followed what the Bible says by eating fruits and vegetables. I was eating mostly raw vegetables. I found out that the bitter fruits and vegetables were better for my body, for they are alkaline. I also followed some of the Gerson cancer therapy protocols. My friend, Dr. Siton, who has a holistic physical therapy practice in Houston, Texas, taught me how to eat healthy. She taught me how to follow Gerson protocols such as juicing, coffee enema, choosing supplements and vitamins, etc. She also performed physical therapy to cleanse my colon and liver. For about six months, my daily nutrition consisted of green juice (carrots, green apple, and kale or other greens), raw vegetables (bitter melon, cucumber), and cooked vegetables. The Gerson cancer therapy recommended thirteen cups of juice each day. However, I could only take up to six. After that, I started to vomit. Once I started juicing, I could not eat meat, for it was a burden and painful for my liver. I limited or eliminated processed and junk foods. I avoided toxic chemicals such as food coloring, monosodium glutamate (MSG), aluminum, etc. I also eliminated dairy products such as eggs, milk, and butter. In the morning, I drank from four to six cups of juice (carrots, green apple, and kale or other greens) and took all my supplements (e.g., vitamin C, vitamin B, fish oil, COQ10, MSM, etc.). I also ate fresh raw bitter melon. For lunch, I ate soup with green leaves, such as malunggay or spinach, and vegetable salads. I snacked on some fruits that are not sweet. I ate dinner at or before six in the evening. On certain occasions, I would totally skip dinner if I was already full.

CHAPTER 14

Refuge and Fortress

> Whoever dwells in the shelter of the Most High will rest in the shadow of the Almighty. I will say of the Lord, 'He is my refuge and my fortress, my God, in whom I trust.' Surely he will save you from the fowler's snare and from the deadly pestilence.
>
> Psalm 91:1-3

A refuge is "a state of safety, protection, or shelter."[8] A fortress is "a fortified place; a large and permanent fortification, sometimes including a town; a fort; a castle; a stronghold; a place of defense or security."[9] In our lives there are times, events, or situations when we encounter danger or trouble. When danger or trouble comes, such as natural disasters, wars, or accidents, we look for a refuge, a place where we feel safe and protected. In case of a heavy rain, we move to higher ground where we are away from flooding. Then we find a fortress, an actual dwelling, such as a tent or a covered court where we are kept warm and dry from the rain and other elements of the weather.

> *Lord, you are my God*; I will exalt you and praise your name, for in perfect faithfulness you have done wonderful things, things planned long ago...*You have been a refuge for the poor, a refuge for the needy in their distress, a shelter from the storm* and a shade from the heat. For the breath of the ruthless is like a storm driving against a wall and like the heat of the desert. You silence the uproar of foreigners; as heat is reduced by the shadow of a cloud, so the song of the ruthless is stilled.
>
> Isaiah 25:1, 4-5

Understanding this biblical principle that God is our Refuge and Fortress prompted me to seek Him when I encountered danger and trouble.

- Seek God's wisdom to identify when danger and trouble are coming. Prepare a plan.
- Immediately seek refuge and fortress in the Lord God alone. Act on your plan.

> God is our refuge and strength, a very present help in trouble. Therefore will not we fear,

> though the earth be removed, and though the mountains be carried into the midst of the sea; Though the waters thereof roar and be troubled, though the mountains shake with the swelling thereof. There is a river, the streams whereof shall make glad the city of God, the holy place of the tabernacles of the most High. God is in the midst of her; she shall not be moved: God shall help her, and that right early.
>
> Psalm 46:1-5 (KJV)

When my body's cells became abnormal and divided uncontrollably (cancer), a huge storm was brewing inside my body. I sought God's wisdom on how to manage the cancer pain. I asked the Lord God that the cancer pain happen only in the evening when I am at home. I did not want to pass out at work, while driving, or somewhere else. I also asked the Lord God to help me bear the pain. This was the end stage of the cancer, as the cancer already affected several organs (lung, liver, remaining left kidney). The cancer pain was inevitable at this stage. I was prepared to face the battle each day. The metastatic cancer pain felt like I was facing a duel with death each night for eight months. It was beyond comparison to my past pain with cancers and cysts. My first pain with the ovarian cyst was sharp, lasted several hours, and I cried in agony for a couple of days. My second pain with the breast cyst was intermittent, but it brought me into depression. My third pain with the right kidney cancer lasted several years with dull pain that came and went quickly. All these cancers were on the first and second stages, thus the pain was mild and bearable.

> The eternal God is your refuge, and underneath are the everlasting arms. He will drive out your enemies before you, saying, "Destroy them!"
>
> Deuteronomy 33:27

> For in the time of trouble he shall hide me in his pavilion: in the secret of his tabernacle shall he hide me; he shall set me up upon a rock.
>
> Psalm 27:5, KJV

Prepare a Plan - My doctors discourage their patients in taking pain medication, for it will affect the liver. They advised me to take it only if the pain was not bearable. Thank God, who is my first source in everything. I consulted Him on what to do, how to act, what to follow, and just about anything.

Between seven to eight in the evening, I needed to be in bed waiting to fight the cancer pain battle. I prayed to the Lord God, confessed all my sins, and asked for forgiveness. I surrendered everything to the Lord and Savior, especially my life. I then asked the Lord God to be my Refuge and Fortress (stronghold). I asked Him to protect, shield, and carry my frail body. I also asked Him to fight the battle for me and give me the victory in the name of Jesus and by the blood of Jesus.

> Trust in him at all times, you people; pour out your hearts to him, *for God is our refuge*.
>
> Psalm 62:8

> The Lord is my rock, my fortress and my deliverer; my God is my rock, in whom I take refuge, my shield and the horn of my salvation, my stronghold.
>
> Psalm 18:2

Act on Your Plan - Shortly after my prayer, the cancer pain came like a lighted saber, attacking my liver then my head. God is trustworthy and faithful. He is the God who fought all my battles with cancer pain. Immediately, the pain was gone in less than five seconds. I was already knocked down from the pain. At this time, the Lord God carried me into His loving arms; He protected me, and He shielded me from the pain and agony. The Lord God let me sleep in His bosom the whole night through. Then the Lord God woke me up early in the morning at the crack of dawn. I felt renewed and refreshed. It was like my body was rebooted like a computer. It was new again. Surely God's mercies are new every morning. Thank God, who is my Refuge and Fortress. What a victory! Hallelujah!

> I long to dwell in your tent forever and *take refuge in the shelter of your wings.*
>
> Psalm 61:4

> Lord, my strength and my fortress, *my refuge in time of distress*, to you the nations will come from the ends of the earth and say, "Our ancestors possessed nothing but false gods, worthless idols that did them no good."
>
> Jeremiah 16:19

CHAPTER 15

Enter God's Rest

> Observe the Sabbath, because it is holy to you. Anyone who desecrates it is to be put to death; those who do any work on that day must be cut off from their people. For six days work is to be done, but the seventh day is a day of sabbath rest, holy to the Lord. Whoever does any work on the Sabbath day is to be put to death. The Israelites are to observe the Sabbath, celebrating it for the generations to come as a lasting covenant. It will be a sign between Me and the Israelites forever, for in six days the Lord made the heavens and the earth, and on the seventh day He rested and was refreshed.
>
> Exodus 31:14-17

God created the heavens and the earth for six days. On the seventh day, God rested from all His work. God blessed the seventh day and made it holy because on it, He rested from all the work of creating that He had done (Genesis 2:2). God also commanded man to follow

Him—work for six days and rest on the seventh day. God promised man that he would be refreshed if he follows it, and if he does not, he will be put to death. Understanding this biblical principle taught me to enter God's rest as He commanded us.

- Remember and observe Sabbath rest (Exodus 20:8-11).
- Lie down and sleep daily (Psalm 4:8).

God requires us to be obedient to His commands. As I meditated on God's words and this commandment, I realized that I was disobedient to the Lord God. I asked the Lord for forgiveness. Then I asked the Lord to teach me His ways. As a working wife and mother, I easily forget this commandment. I worked as an internal auditor for a financial services firm in San Antonio, Texas. We worked five days a week. We also had work from home (WFH) opportunities. However, there were weeks when I work more than forty hours. As a wife and mother, there were also errands to run and chores to be done at home. I am so blessed that my husband Joesel helped me with most of the household chores. Then there were also extra-curricular activities volunteering in the community: church Bible study co-leader, professional organization leader, and Filipino community nonprofit leader. I enjoyed doing it so much, that sometimes I overdid it. Rest and sleep were the two things that suffered most.

As a child I learned from Sunday School about the commandment,

> "Remember the Sabbath day
> by keeping it holy."

However, I did not practice it. My family and the church I attended did not practice it in the Philippines. Saturday, which is Sabbath, was the day we did all the household chores and other extra-curricular and social activities. When I moved to Germany and then later the United States, the churches that I attended did not practice it. However, there was an Air Force Chaplain at the Fairchild Air Force Base in Washington, who taught us a discipleship class. He, his wife, and children practiced the Sabbath rest. They just stayed home and rested—no work, no television, no errands, and no chores. It was a time of communing with God. Wow! I was impressed. That was a powerful testimony I heard about Sabbath rest; it was remembered and observed. To God be the glory! I also heard from other pastors that since Saturday and Sunday were the busiest days of the week for them, they chose another day of the week, such as Monday, as their Sabbath rest, which was also their day off. I prayed to the Holy Spirit for guidance. There were days that my Sabbath rest with the Lord was on Saturday. There were also other days of the week that I observed Sabbath rest. There was no consistent day. This is an area of my life that I am constantly working.

> The Lord God took the man and put him in the Garden of Eden to work it and take care of it.
>
> Genesis 2:15

Even today, we continue to work and take care of God's creation. This is our purpose. At the end of the day, our work takes a toll on our bodies. We get tired from all our labor. Our Creator made us this way. He left us instructions on how to take care of our bodies after a day's work: at night we need to lie down and sleep. The Lord God heals and restores us when our bodies are resting and asleep. He is truly the Lord God our Healer. The next morning, we feel rested, refreshed, restored, and recharged. We are again ready for another day.

> I lay down and slept, yet I woke up in safety, for the Lord was watching over me.
>
> Psalm 3:5, NLT

> In peace I will lie down and sleep, for you alone, O Lord, will keep me safe.
>
> Psalm 4:8, NLT

During my cancer battle from 2014 to 2015, my body was already weak. The cancer pains brought me anguish, anxiety, and stress. The Lord God our Healer is merciful. The pain only happened at night around seven or eight. The pain lasted only a few seconds from the liver to the brain. Then the Lord God made me sleep and carried me into His arms. The Lord God gave my body rest from all the pains, restored every single cell, refreshed me with new strength, and recharged me with new energy. While I was sleeping, the Lord God was working. Bible verses from the Psalm of David that I prophesy over my life strengthens me.

> The Lord is my shepherd; I shall not want. He maketh me to lie down in green pastures: He leadeth me beside the still waters. He restoreth my soul: He leadeth me in the paths of righteousness for His name's sake. Yea, though I walk through the valley of the shadow of death, I will fear no evil: for thou art with Me; Thy rod and Thy staff they comfort me.
>
> Psalm 23:1-4 (KJV)

I woke up each morning ready for a new day doing what God wants me to do. What a miracle-working God we have! To God be the glory!

CHAPTER 16

Walking in the Light

> This is the message we have heard from Him and declare to you: God is light; in Him there is no darkness at all. If we claim to have fellowship with Him and yet walk in the darkness, we lie and do not live out the truth. But if we walk in the light, as He is in the light, we have fellowship with one another, and the blood of Jesus, His Son, purifies us from all sin.
>
> 1 John 1:5-7

Darkness means sin. Sin means we are separated from God. Even if we claim that we have fellowship with God, but we do not walk in His light, then we are still in darkness. Understanding this biblical principle helped me see myself in a new light. It taught me to focus on the Lord Jesus, the Light of the world, who purifies me from all sin.

- Daily, read God's Word, which is a lamp for my feet and a light on my path (Psalm 119:105).

- Daily, follow God's words and laws (Psalm 119:106).

The Lord God requires us to walk with Him daily. Reading the Bible, believing in God, and following all His commands and decrees help us to walk in God's light. His light gives us joy. Walking in the light of God is a lifestyle. It is a process that we perform daily. We walk and live our lives in alignment with the Word of God. Daily walking in the light indicates growth and progress. Daily walking in the light leads us towards our spiritual maturity. By God's power and grace, we walk daily in His light.

> For ye were sometimes in darkness, but now are ye light in the Lord: walk as children of light.
>
> Ephesians 5:8, KJV

I received the Lord Jesus as my Savior and Lord when I was seven years old. However, there were areas in my life that I allowed darkness to creep into my life and dwell as a sin, such as fear. Fear is an emotion that can affect the function of the kidneys. In 2012 after being involved in several car accidents, fear and shock engulfed me so much that it affected my daily living. There were days that I did not want to go out of the house and drive my car. I even carpooled with my husband for several weeks. In February 2014, I was finally diagnosed with kidney cancer, where my right kidney was affected. Then in November 2014, I was diagnosed again with another cancer affecting the remaining left kidney. I knew I had to align my life with the Word of God regarding fear. I knew that fear is not of God. Continuous fear is not of God. I renounced fear. I decided to live in alignment with the Word of God.

"For God hath not given us the spirit of fear; but of power, and of love, and of a sound mind" (2 Timothy 1:7, KJV).

Here are the steps I followed overcome fear:

- Ask the Lord God for forgiveness over fear.
- Believe in the Lord Jesus, who is the Light of the world (John 8:12).
- Follow the Lord Jesus so you will have the light of life (John 8:12).
- Daily, declare the Word of God to remove fear, and trust in the Lord God.

> God is our refuge and strength, an ever-present help in trouble. Therefore we will not fear, though the earth give way and the mountains fall into the heart of the sea, though its waters roar and foam and the mountains quake with their surging.
>
> Psalm 46:1-3

> And the Lord said unto Joshua, "Fear them not: for I have delivered them into thine hand; there shall not a man of them stand before thee."
>
> Joshua 10:8, KJV

> *Fear thou not; for I am with thee:* be not dismayed; for I am thy God: I will strengthen thee; yea, I will help thee; yea, I will uphold thee with the right hand of my righteousness.
>
> Isaiah 41:10, KJV

> But I said to you, *"Do not be shocked, nor fear them."*
>
> Deuteronomy 1:29, NASB

> Be strong and courageous. *Do not fear or be in dread of them, for it is the Lord your God who goes with you.* He will not leave you or forsake you.
>
> Deuteronomy 31:6

> *The Lord is my light and my salvation; whom shall I fear?* The Lord is the stronghold of my life; of whom shall I be afraid.
>
> Psalm 27:1, KJV

Praise the Lord! I overcame darkness. The next step is to show to the world how God's light made me walk from darkness to light.

> Let your light so shine before men, that they may see your good works, and glorify your Father which is in heaven.
>
> Matthew 5:16, KJV

Read Psalm 91. This chapter is very powerful. Memorize it. Recite it. Sing it in a song. Whatever you do, it will lift up your spirit, filled with love, power, and sound mind.

> Whoever dwells in the shelter of the Most High will rest in the shadow of the Almighty. I will say of the Lord, "He is my refuge and my fortress, my God, in whom I trust." Surely He will save you from the fowler's snare and from the deadly pestilence. He will cover you with his feathers, and under His wings you will find refuge; His faithfulness will be your shield and rampart. You will not fear the terror of night, nor the arrow that flies by day, nor the pestilence that stalks in the darkness, nor the plague that destroys at midday. A thousand may fall at your side, ten thousand at your right hand, but it will not come near you. You will only observe with your eyes and see the punishment of the wicked. If you say,

"The Lord is my refuge," and you make the Most High your dwelling, no harm will overtake you, no disaster will come near your tent. For he will command his angels concerning you to guard you in all your ways; they will lift you up in their hands, so that you will not strike your foot against a stone. You will tread on the lion and the cobra; you will trample the great lion and the serpent. "Because he loves me," says the Lord, "I will rescue him; I will protect him, for he acknowledges my name. He will call on me, and I will answer him; I will be with him in trouble, I will deliver him and honor him. With long life I will satisfy him and show him my salvation."

Psalm 91 (KJV)

CHAPTER 17

Joy of the Lord

> Nehemiah said, "Go and enjoy choice food and sweet drinks, and send some to those who have nothing prepared. This day is holy to our Lord. Do not grieve, for *the joy of the Lord is your strength*."
>
> Nehemiah 8:10

Being stricken with cancer twice in one year brought me great sadness. I cried hard after the oncologist told me of the news. I did not go back to work that afternoon. I cried out to the Lord my God. I was not prepared to face another cancer. The merriment of Christmas that year in 2014 did not even lift me up. I did not even take pleasure in the food and drinks that season. In fact, I did not have any appetite. My body was already at its lowest level of energy. It was like the last flicker of light from the candlestick that is about to fade away. I was facing death every night that I was knocked out from cancer pain. I was also silently retreating from the crowd.

However, every morning brought me great joy when I woke up alive. God's mercies are truly new every morning. Having enough strength to get out of bed gave me new hope each day. Understanding the biblical principle about the joy of the Lord, and living it every day, was a great and fulfilling exercise of my spiritual strength. It taught me to focus on Him, my Healer.

- The Lord is my daily inspiration for good pleasure and true happiness.
- The Lord opens my eyes daily to show me the wonderful world He created for me to enjoy.
- Daily, I accept the gift of joy from the Lord.
- Daily, I verbally appreciated the Lord's goodness, mercies, and love.

When I was a child, I woke up with anticipation for a fun and enjoyable day. My father, Alaric, wanted us children to enjoy our childhood days. He was not strict with the school homework assignments, nor the household chores. I asked him one day for the reason. He said that he experienced growing up during World War II in hiding. There were times that they had to stay quiet to keep the enemies away from their families and to keep them alive. He did not want us to experience that unhappy, fearful, and sad life. He wanted us to make wonderful and joyful memories during our childhood. When I went home to Oroquieta City from March to July 2015, my Papa Alaric's words resonated in my heart. I decided to find my daily inspiration from the Lord God my Father. I prayed that the Lord would send me people that would lift up my spirit that day. When I walked in the city plaza each morning, I met some familiar people. Some of my Papa Alaric's families greeted me each morning. Sometimes I joined Uncle Ting, my father's brother, and his wife, Auntie Lilia, for a thirty-minute walk in the city plaza. I remembered him saying that he heard from the American television that it is good to walk at least thirty minutes a day for good health. Auntie Day, my Papa Alaric's only sister, also walked with me along the shoreline to breathe in the refreshing sea breeze. Auntie Cora, the wife of Uncle Eric, my father's brother, also walked with me in the morning going up and down our street. We were greeted by our friendly neighbors along the way. On some days, Christy and Sally also spent time with my early morning walk. On some days, my sister Annemarie and her husband Ernesto would walk with me around our neighborhood. Then in the afternoon, I enjoyed the daily chat with our neighbors which included Uncle Jun, my Papa Alaric's fourth brother, and his wife, Auntie Lina, as well as Auntie Cora and another neighbor. We enjoyed just chatting outside and seeing people pass by.

My sister Annemarie is a practicing lawyer in the Philippines, like our father Attorney Alaric Pena Acosta.

She also had out-of-town legal cases. She let me accompany her and her husband, Ernesto, on out-of-town legal cases. It was also reminiscent of my childhood days when our Papa Alaric brought us along with him on his out-of-town legal cases. I looked forward to each trip with anticipation, watching the beautiful green countryside scenery of fresh provincial air, enjoying the places and people we met, and savoring the good delicacies of the towns and cities we visited.

Another enjoyable thing we did as a family is vacationing together. During our childhood, my Papa Alaric and Mommy Lydia planned out-of-town trips each year. We looked forward to each trip, especially going to the big cities like Manila and Cebu. The fun and exciting part was of course the travel itself, especially riding the plane or the boat. We also enjoyed going to the mall, shopping, and eating in fancy restaurants that were not found in our city or province. We also took time to visit some favorite tourist spots or visit some friends and relatives in the city. When I visited my hometown from March to July of 2015, my parents were no longer with us, for they were already resting in the Lord our Creator. Our oldest sister Annemarie and her husband Ernesto planned out-of-town family trips. In tow were our three younger brothers with their families: Jose with his wife, Det, and children, Ella and Josh; Aldric with his wife,

Jennifer, and son, AJ; and Cedric with his wife, Christy, and son, CJ.

Accepting this daily gift of joy from the Lord truly gave me strength. I appreciated the time and the people that the Lord God put on my path, who brought me joy and lifted my spirit up. Little did these people know that they encouraged and strengthened me each day. They were doing good deeds each day. They accepted me as my own person. They did not question my illness. They let me join their circle. I felt I belong. I thank God for that gift of being loved.

CHAPTER 18

Healing Oils of the Bible

> They drove out many demons and anointed many sick people with oil and healed them.
>
> Mark 6:13

Healing oils were used both in the Old and New Testament times for anointing, healing, and more. The gifts of the Lord Jesus from the two of the Three Kings were frankincense and myrrh.

When I was about nineteen years old, I was diagnosed with juvenile arthritis due to joint pain, swelling, and stiffness. On its first attack, I was in bed for three days. The doctor told me not to take too much pain medication for it can easily harm my liver. The Gerson cancer therapy book that I followed in March 2015 also mentions to find alternative medicine to deal with cancer pain, as traditional pain medications will affect the liver.

I remembered the Bible and the healing oils they used from ancient times. I used essential oils for anointing and healing. I surrendered everything, including my life, to the Lord at the end of each day. I prayed that the Lord God heal me and protect me as the cancer pain attacked my body, especially the liver and head. I then prayed over the essential oils that I used for anointing over my liver and head. Then the cancer pain knocked me down in a couple of seconds. The next morning, I awoke feeling rested, refreshed, renewed, and restored. God gave me this daily miracle. To God be the glory!

Here are the essential oils I used for anointing. They are all therapeutic grade essential oils.

- *Aloes (Sandalwood)* – Also called oil of joy and gladness. It was used for Jesus' embalming (John 19:39).
- *Cassia* – One of the ingredients of the sacred anointing oil (Exodus 30:22-29).
- *Cedarwood* – Used for healing skin disease like leprosy (Leviticus 14:3-7).
- *Frankincense* – One of the ingredients of the fragrant blend of incense (Exodus 30:34-35).
- *Galbanum* – One of the ingredients of the fragrant blend of incense (Exodus 30:34-35).
- *Hyssop* – Used for healing skin disease like leprosy (Leviticus 14:3-7).

- *Myrrh* – One of the ingredients of the sacred anointing oil (Exodus 30:22-29).
- *Myrtle* – The branches were used as temporary shelters which is also a sign of recovery (Nehemiah 8:15). The essential oil is used for respiratory illnesses and to calm anxiety and tension.
- *Onycha* - One of the ingredients of the fragrant blend of incense (Exodus 30:34-35).
- *Rose of Sharon (Cistus)* – Considered a spiritual oil (Song of Songs 2:1).
- *Spikenard* – Used for perfume and embalming (Mark 14:3).
- *Cypress* – Used for cleansing wounds (Isaiah 44:14).

My good friend Lorna introduced me to essential oils. When I was sick with cancer, Lorna introduced to me the "Twelve Oils of Ancient Scriptures" that were of therapeutic grade. I used these oils to anoint myself on or before the cancer pain that attacked me in the evening. Later, I mixed all the essential oils in a bottle. I just anointed myself with the essential oils when I was alone in my bedroom in the Philippines. These essential oils have different healing properties, which include enhancing quality deep sleep, relaxing the body, reducing stress, clearing the mind, calming anxiety and tension, supporting cellular function, supporting the nervous, respiratory, and circulatory systems, easing pain and swelling, and more.

I also attended the class of Dr. Stewart, PhD about the Chemistry of Essential Oils in July 2017 in Dallas, Texas. Since there were only a few less than a dozen who attended this class, Dr. Stewart even discussed to us briefly about the healing oils of the Bible. Mrs. Stewart had just finished her cancer treatment at that time. They both shared the cancer healing journey as a patient and caregiver when they were both admitted to a natural cancer treatment facility overseas. They shared about the Lord God's miracle healing for both of them. Dr. Stewart also shared the gift of knowledge about essential oils that he studied and learned about over the years. It was a blessing to attend that class with Dr. and Mrs. Stewart.

CHAPTER 19

Church Fellowship

> That which was from the beginning, which we have heard, which we have seen with our eyes, which we have looked at and our hands have touched—this we proclaim concerning the Word of life. The life appeared; we have seen it and testify to it, and we proclaim to you the eternal life, which was with the Father and has appeared to us. We proclaim to you what we have seen and heard, so that you also may have fellowship with us. And our fellowship is with the Father and with his Son, Jesus Christ.
>
> 1 John 1:1-3

When I was sick, I felt tired to the point that I did not want to go out. I preferred to stay at home, away from the hustle and bustle of everyday life. I wanted to preserve the flicker of energy left in my physical body. This however, brought me to darkness and depression. I felt so lonely and alone. I know the Lord God was always with me, and I know that He will never leave me nor forsake me. The Word of Life (Jesus) is the Savior and Lord of my life. He is the Lord Jesus who gave me eternal life. During these darkest of days, the Lord God reminded me of this biblical principle while I am still living on earth.

- Live in unity with God's people daily, for there the Lord bestows His blessing, even life forevermore (Psalm 133:1, 3).
- Meet with God's people daily to motivate and encourage each other (Hebrews 10:24-25).

We are God's temple, and God's Spirit dwells in our midst. God's temple is sacred. During those days, I gathered all my strength to attend church services and Bible study meetings. I even accepted house visits and fellowship from church members. The Bible says that when two or three are gathered in the name of Lord Jesus, He is in our midst (Matthew 18:20). The declaration of God's healing power, the sharing of testimony of God's healing, and sharing the Word of God motivates, encourages, and gives us strength. As I heard the Word of God, I received it with joy. It quickened my spirit. It was like a fuel that increased my energy. My spirit was filled with the power of the Holy Spirit.

When I arrived in the Philippines in March 2015, I attended the Only Jesus Fellowship, a home church located in my parents' residence in Oroquieta City. We met twice each week on Sunday afternoon and Wednesday evening. Pastor Ngalot or Brother Ernesto led and delivered the message during each service. They always prayed for the needs of the members, especially healing. They prayed for my healing every time. I felt the healing touch of God that strengthened me each day.

Churches should have regular healing services. Many people are tired, sick, and weary as we live our daily lives. When I was a child, I asked my Papa Alaric why we always go to church on Sundays (nothing missed). He answered that the church is a hospital for God's people. People worked for six days. People get tired, sick, and weary. That is why on Sundays, we go to church to ask the Lord God to heal us and keep us healthy all week long. What a beautiful testimony. This biblical principle of church fellowship stuck to my spirit. When I was an adult living away from the parents in the city, and when I missed a Sunday church, I immediately felt a weakness in my spirit and body. Immediately, I would attend the mid-week service or the next Sunday worship. What a powerful testimony of God's healing power and grace.

I also remembered our Mommy Lydia bringing us to church and other church fellowship and gatherings when there were healing services from guest preachers or pastors. One day in 1997, my Mommy Lydia asked me to jump into the car, for they were heading to a healing service at Nestleigh Beach Resort by Pastor Al, a traveling missionary from California, USA. My Mommy Lydia had just had one of her kidneys removed due to cancer in April 1997. This was the year when my husband Joesel was assigned to one year in South Korea by the US Air Force. My children and I stayed with my parents in the Philippines to help me and the children overcome anxiety separation from my husband. We were late during the service and sat at the very end of the room. During the service, the Holy Spirit asked Pastor Al to call someone with a broken heart who needed healing. Some people came up, who asked for prayer and healing. The Holy Spirit kept telling Pastor Al to call someone out in the back. Finally, he pointed at me, the lady who was seated at the back. As I was kneeling in the front, my spirit felt the healing touch of the Lord. I was crying my heart out. It felt like the Holy Spirit pulled a knife out of my heart. I remember Dr. Al saying that the Lord God healed my broken heart. What a miracle-healing God.

While still in Ramstein AFB, Germany in late 1994, and in the process of transferring to Spokane, Washington, there were cysts found on my breasts. This freaked me out. I had just had an operation on my left ovary to remove the cysts in December 1992. We arrived in Spokane, Washington in November 1994. All the follow-up for my breast exams were done at Fairchild AFB hospital. I was scared and anxious, not only for the result of the follow-up breast exam, but also adjusting to the new environment. I was overwhelmed of the transfer process from Germany to Spokane, USA. I was brokenhearted to learn of another disease. One morning while my husband Joesel was at work, I remember the evil spirit trying to harm my body and my daughters. I asked the Lord to remove the evil spirit and not harm me or my two daughters. Immediately, the evil spirit left me and never came back. I thank God for the immediate deliverance that day. Hallelujah!

A few months later, my husband Joesel and I found a church at Fairchild Air Force Base, where we attended the Sunday services. I also joined the Wednesday prayer meetings. I remember the first time I attended the Wednesday prayer meeting, I felt the ground shake like an earthquake. I was filled with amazement at God's power that evening. I also experienced the power of the children of God coming together, praying for one another, breaking down bondages, and encouraging each other. I felt I belonged in the family of God in a new land. God healed me and made me whole. Hallelujah!

> Therefore encourage one another and build each other up, just as in fact you are doing.
>
> 1 Thessalonians 5:11

...that is, that you and I may be mutually encouraged by each other's faith.

Romans 1:12

Two are better than one, because they have a good return for their labor: If either of them falls down, one can help the other up. But pity anyone who falls and has no one to help them up.

Ecclesiastes 4:9-10

CHAPTER 20

Restoration

> Create in me a clean heart, O God; and renew a right spirit within me. Cast me not away from Thy presence; and take not Thy holy spirit from me. Restore unto me the joy of Thy salvation; and uphold me with Thy free spirit. Then will I teach transgressors Thy ways; and sinners shall be converted unto Thee.
>
> Psalm 51:10-13 (KJV)

Per Merriam-Webster Dictionary, restore means to "give back, return," and restoration means "an act of restoring or the condition of being restored: such as a bringing back to a former position or condition: reinstatement."[10 11]

In the Bible, restoration means replacing what was lost to the point that it is sometimes greater than the original. This is true in the story of Job where he lost his fortunes. Later, the Lord restored his fortunes and gave him twice as much as he had before. "After Job had prayed for his friends, the Lord restored his fortunes and gave him twice as much as he had before" (Job 42:10).

Tell God's People that He is the Lord God the Healer - In December 2015, I asked the Lord God, "Why two cancers in a year?" He replied, "I want you to tell My people that I am the Lord God the Healer." This is my testimony of the healing power of the Lord God the Healer. He alone can heal us completely. He alone can restore us to the previous state of being as a healthy person. He alone can make us walk in divine health. Jesus came that we may have life and have it to the fullest.

> The thief comes only to steal and kill and destroy; I have come that they may have life and have it to the full.
>
> John 10:10

Kidney Cancer Healing - After the surgery to remove my right kidney that was affected with cancer, my doctor, Dr. Tecuanhuey (Urologist/Surgeon), told me that the cancer was encapsulated and did not spread to the other organs. That was great news. By faith I believed that I was completely healed.

Nightly Cancer Pain and Healing - In November 2014, nine months after my kidney cancer surgery, Dr. Kapoor

(Oncologist) told me to obtain a CT scan to check that the cancer did not recur or spread. The CT scan spotted a nodule in my right lung and cysts in the liver and remaining left kidney. I became weaker as the months passed after the kidney surgery. I prayed before that any cancer pain would not occur during the day, as what I experienced with my left ovary in 1992, my breast in 1994, and the kidney in 2014. God is faithful. By December 2014, I experienced nightly cancer pains from the liver to the head that knocked me down from evening to the next morning. I woke up refreshed, renewed, and restored the next morning. That was my daily healing miracle. God is good. He sustained me each day.

Cancer Pain Completely Gone - The cancer pain was unbearable after seven months of mostly nightly pains. I felt the pain in my heart being broken down into two. One evening in July 2015, I asked the Lord to take me or heal me, for it was unbearable. Then I saw God's golden and shining hand coming over to touch me. I grabbed it immediately and placed it over my liver. The Lord God the Healer touched me and healed me completely from cancer. What a miracle. The nightly cancer pain from my liver to my head was completely gone by July 2015. Indeed, God is a miracle-working God.

By July 2015, I went back home to San Antonio, Texas for my oncology follow-up. The oncologist read the CT scan result and said, "The CT scan result is beautiful. There is no more trace of cancer." Praise the Lord! God is a miracle-healing God.

Overall Strength Restored - By October 2015, I consulted an endodontist to have my left root canal tooth removed completely. I also had my amalgam fillings removed and changed to white fillings. Immediately, I noticed that the weakness in my body was gone. Previously, I felt an overall low energy level. I felt weak all the time. I barely had the energy to wake up each morning and do my daily tasks, such as reading my Bible, taking care of myself, eating, and walking. Now, my energy is restored. To God be the glory! That was another miracle healing from the Lord God my Healer.

> I will not die but live, and will proclaim what the Lord has done.
>
> Psalm 118:17

I will tell God's people that He is the Lord God the Healer. Truly, I will not die but live and proclaim what the Lord has done to me. I will build the hospital in the Philippines for the Lord God the Healer.

PART III:

INVITATION TO RECEIVE THE LORD GOD THE HEALER

Part III

Praise the Lord! You finally reached the last part of this book. I am very grateful that you read the whole book. You can read this book again and again. As I previously mentioned, you can use this book to strengthen and encourage you. You can also use this book as a guide when you, or a family member, or a friend, or a caretaker is battling with cancer or any kind of sickness or disease. God is faithful to His words. He is the Lord God the Healer. He heals all our sicknesses and diseases. The Lord God the Healer is the only One who can heal us completely—body, soul, and spirit.

CHAPTER 21

Return to the Lord

> Come, let us *return to the Lord*. He has torn us to pieces but He will *heal* us; He has injured us but He will bind up our wounds. After two days He will *revive us*; on the third day He will *restore* us, that we may live in His presence. Let us *acknowledge the Lord*; let us press on to acknowledge Him. As surely as the sun rises, He will appear; He will come to us like the winter rains, like the spring rains that water the earth.
>
> Hosea 6:1-3

Today, I invite all of you to return to the Lord. He alone is the Lord who heals, binds up our wounds, revives, and restores. Let us acknowledge the Lord God the Healer.

> Surely He took up our pain and bore our suffering, yet we considered Him punished by God, stricken by Him, and afflicted. But He

> was pierced for our transgressions, He was crushed for our iniquities; the punishment that brought us peace was on Him, and by His wounds we are healed.
>
> Isaiah 53:4-5

The Prophet Isaiah prophesied about the only begotten Son, who took up our pain and bore or suffering, for by His wounds we are healed. Then Peter preached about the only begotten Son, Jesus Christ, that the Prophet Isaiah prophesied about. Peter was one of Jesus' disciples who witnessed His ministry here on Earth.

> When they hurled their insults at Him, He did not retaliate; when He suffered, He made no threats. Instead, He entrusted Himself to Him who judges justly. "He himself bore our sins" in His body on the cross, so that we might die to sins and live for righteousness; "*by His wounds you have been healed.*" For "you were like sheep going astray," but now *you have returned to the Shepherd and Overseer of your souls.*
>
> 1 Peter 2:23-25

Today, I invite all of you to return to the Lord. He is the Shepherd and Overseer of our souls. He alone can heal us and heal us completely.

Say the prayer below to invite the Lord Jesus into your heart to be your Savior and Lord.

"Lord Jesus, I am a sinner.
Forgive me of all my sins.
Come into my heart.
Be my Lord and Savior.
Be my Lord God my Healer.
Write my name in the Lamb's Book of Life.
Thank you for the gift of eternal life.
Amen."

Bibliography

Henschke, Claudia I., Peggy McMarthy, and Sarah Wernick. *Lung Cancer: Myths, Facts, Choices—and Hope.* New York, NY: W.W. Norton & Company, Inc., 2003.

"How Much Water Should You Drink Every Day?" WebMD. Accessed August 8, 2022. https://www.webmd.com/diet/how-much-water-to-drink#:~:text=For%20men%2C%20the%20Institute%20of,10%20cups%20of%20water%20daily.

Leaf, Caroline. *Who Switched off My Brain?: Controlling Toxic Thoughts and Emotions.* Dallas, Texas: Inprov. Ltd., 2009.

"Refuge vs Shelter - What's the Difference?" WikiDiff, June 14, 2022. https://wikidiff.com/refuge/shelter.

www.merriam-webster.com. "Definition of RESTORATION." Accessed August 2, 2022. https://www.merriam-webster.com/dictionary/restoration.

www.merriam-webster.com. "Definition of RESTORE." Accessed August 2, 2022. https://www.merriam-webster.com/dictionary/restore.

Endnotes

1 Caroline Leaf, *Who Switched off My Brain?: Controlling Toxic Thoughts and Emotions* (Dallas, Texas: Inprov. Ltd., 2009), 13.

2 Ibid, 14.

3 Ibid, 8.

4 Ibid, 19-20.

5 Claudia I. Henschke, Peggy McMarthy, and Sarah Wernick, *Lung Cancer: Myths, Facts, Choices—and Hope* (New York, NY: W.W. Norton & Company, Inc., 2003), 117.

6 "How Much Water Should You Drink Every Day?" WebMD, accessed August 8, 2022, https://www.webmd.com/diet/how-much-water-to-drink#:~:text=For%20men%2C%20the%20Institute%20of,10%20cups%20of%20water%20daily.

7 Ibid.

8 "Refuge vs Shelter - What's the Difference?," WikiDiff, June 14, 2022, https://wikidiff.com/refuge/shelter.

9 Ibid.

10 "Definition of RESTORE," www.merriam-webster.com, accessed August 2, 2022, https://www.merriam-webster.com/dictionary/restore.

11 "Definition of RESTORATION," www.merriam-webster.com, accessed August 2, 2022, https://www.merriam-webster.com/dictionary/restoration.

CPSIA information can be obtained
at www.ICGtesting.com
Printed in the USA
JSHW081111041122
32563JS00009B/10

9 798887 380193